SCHOLASTIC

D0534496

Teaching Grammar
With Perfect Poems
for Middle School

Nancy Mack

New York • Toronto • London • Auckland • Sydney
Mexico City • New Delhi • Hong Kong • Buenos Aires

Teaching *Resources*

Credits

"Hurray! Hurray! It's New Year's Day!" © 2000 by Kenn Nesbitt. Reprinted by permission of the author. All rights reserved.

"Archie B. McCall" is reprinted from *The New Kid on the Block* by Jack Prelutsky © 1984 by Jack Prelutsky. Used by permission of HarperCollins Publishers.

"I Am Wunk" and "We Moved About a Week Ago" are reprinted from *Something Big Has Been Here* by Jack Prelutsky © 1990 by Jack Prelutsky. Used by permission of HarperCollins Publishers.

"I Remember" by Jana Turner © 2005. Reprinted by permission of the author.

"Three Wishes" from *Near The Window Tree* © 1975, 1980 by Karla Kuskin. Used by permission of Scott Treimel NY.

"Dumb and Dumber" © 2000 by Bruce Lansky. Reprinted from *If Pigs Could Fly—and Other Deep Thoughts: A Collection of Poems*. Used by permission of Meadowbrook Press.

"Harriet Tubman" by Sharon Lindsey © 2006. Reprinted by permission of the author.

"I Will Never Completely Grow Up" by Sara Britton © 2005. Reprinted by permission of the author.

"My Noisy Brother" © 1994 by Bruce Lansky. Reprinted from *My Dog Ate My Homework!* Used by permission of Meadowbrook Press.

Scholastic Inc. grants teachers permission to photocopy the reproducible pages from this book for classroom use. No other part of this publication may be reproduced in whole or in part, or stored in a retrieval system, or transmitted in any form or by any means, electronic, mechanical, photocopying, recording, or otherwise, without written permission of the publisher. For information regarding permission, write to Scholastic Inc., 557 Broadway, New York, NY 10012.

Editor: Sarah Longhi
Cover design: Brian LaRossa
Interior design: Kelli Thompson
Illustrations: Mike Moran

ISBN-13: 978-0-439-92332-3
ISBN-10: 0-439-92332-8
Copyright © 2008 by Nancy Mack.

All rights reserved. Published by Scholastic.
Printed in the U.S.A.
4 5 6 7 8 9 10   31   15 14 13 12 11

Contents

Introduction

Writing the first volume, *Teaching Grammar With Playful Poems*, and sharing it with teachers was a joyous experience for me. Teachers who have read it tell me that they have discovered a new way to think about language instruction: searching for patterns rather than emphasizing errors. Soon after its publication, I became eager to apply my approach to higher-level grammar concepts and sentence structures that many middle-school writers find confusing, such as how to distinguish compound from complex sentences. I found plenty of material. In fact, the hardest part of writing this second volume was limiting myself to one poem per chapter—there are many excellent choices for each grammar concept, as you and your students will find. The poems and formats I selected got the most positive responses from students in grades 5 through 8.

As in the first volume, you'll find follow-up guided poetry-writing activities that reinforce and extend the grammar concepts. I also suggest simple, creative ways for students to publish and present their writing to real audiences, putting their writing in a meaningful context. I hope that as you work with these lessons, you will adapt the ideas to the specific needs of your students and the unique challenges of your learning environment.

About This Book

The teaching strategies I describe in this book are not the only way to teach grammar; they are simply one way I have discovered that really works. These particular strategies were developed after years of my frustrations as a middle-school teacher with a wide range of ineffective methods such as workbook exercises, individualized learning packets, cartoon illustrations, dramatic skits, and humorous example sentences. I may have succeeded in making grammar cute, but I still needed to work on improving student performance.

I pursued this topic further in a two-volume dissertation about cultural preferences for traditional grammar instruction. I discovered that traditional teaching methods are amazingly persistent. To illustrate this point in a nontraditional teaching context, the inmate students whom I taught through a prison program asked me if I had been fired from a regular teaching position since I had asked them to write essays rather than fill out grammar worksheets. Their expectations were that "doing English" meant single-underlining subjects and double-underlining verbs, not engaging in the actual writing of essays. Yet with all my instructional experimentation and study, I still found it a challenge to teach grammar explicitly in the context of meaningful writing. The example lessons described here were refined over a long period of time as I designed discovery mini-lessons, and they will most certainly change again as I learn more about language and teaching.

The challenge of writing a volume about classroom strategies is to design a format that allows teachers to pick and choose, leaving openings for adding, subtracting, and transforming sample activities. I encourage you to try out these strategies, researching what works for you and your students and what needs further innovation. Discuss these strategies with your colleagues and don't forget to ask your students for their reactions.

AN OVERVIEW OF THE LESSONS

In each chapter, you'll find the same lesson format, which includes the following strategies:

- Read aloud a poem with a predictable line pattern and lead students in repeated readings.
- Model the linguistic pattern by writing a class poem.
- Teach the grammar concept through a mini-lesson that names the concept, provides examples, defines and analyzes its function, and links it to a common analogy.
- Help students prewrite ideas for a poem topic, imitate the grammar pattern from a guided writing format, and publish the poem creatively to share with others.
- Engage students in thinking critically about the language patterns and discovering how grammar is used in writing.
- Reinforce grammar concepts with interactive activities.
- Provide extension activities for advanced exploration.
- Explore topic variations and connections to literature.

TIPS FOR IMPLEMENTING THE LESSONS

IMITATION SHOULD PRECEDE DISCUSSIONS ABOUT GRAMMAR.

An error that I made with this type of lesson for years was teaching grammar terms and usage rules first—before doing the writing. Teaching a concept in isolation from its use goes against the way the brain acquires language. Starting with a lecture about grammar also decreases students' engagement and necessitates teaching the whole lesson over again when students need it for the writing task. When teaching these lessons, I purposely hold my linguistic explanations at bay until students almost beg to know what the grammar element highlighted in the model poem is. Teaching the grammar mini-lesson after you've modeled the grammar activity or even after students have written their own pattern poem is a much better course of action than beginning with a lecture.

NEVER TEACH FROM NEGATIVE EXAMPLES.

We may all be tempted to use drill sheets containing sentences with errors to correct or sentences with choices of two forms, one correct and one incorrect. Be aware that these exercises are a particularly unhelpful way to introduce a concept to students because seeing an incorrect model can cause the brain to be confused and overwhelmed. (Similarly, we would not give students math problems worked incorrectly and ask them to guess the correct method from the wrong answers.) The lessons in this book ask students to imitate a grammar pattern offered in a correct and creative model—a strategy that ensures students learn the target grammar concept and perhaps even internalize other concepts such as exceptional word choice and rhyme.

ASK DISCOVERY QUESTIONS TO HELP STUDENTS THINK REFLECTIVELY ABOUT HOW THEY USE LANGUAGE.

Presenting students with models of humorous, rich language and encouraging them to wonder why language works the way it does helps them learn grammar effectively—more effectively than if they're taught the target terms out of context. One important element of the following lessons is the Critical-Thinking Time prompts, which help you initiate a discussion that gets students thinking about how they are learning (metacognitive thinking) and understanding the target grammar concept and related concepts.

The best metacognitive discussions involve spontaneous questioning both from students and from you. The "wondering" thought process clarifies patterns and conventions, helping students make connections to other, more familiar concepts that in turn help them store new information in their long-term memories. This type of open discussion can entice students to become fascinated with language and to experiment with new sentence structures. Keep in mind that people who are fearful of making language mistakes rarely write, and when they do, they use the simplest language possible. We want our students to be daring and masterful writers.

Actively model the wondering process; during your discussions, ask questions to which you do not know the answers. Model looking up information about grammar in reference books such as a dictionary, style book, or thesaurus. Before I started looking things up, I never knew that *most* usually appears with the article *the* or that *eldest* was the preferred superlative form

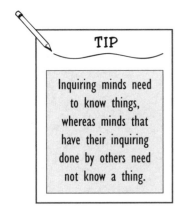

TIP

Inquiring minds need to know things, whereas minds that have their inquiring done by others need not know a thing.

of old. Here are some more questions for which I have recently sought answers: *Is it possible to make a sentence with a comparative adjective without than? What other languages use suffixes? Do all of our suffixes come from Latin?*

ENCOURAGE CREATIVE LANGUAGE USE.

You'll find some students who enjoy coming up with different sentence structures and variations on patterns. Take a moment to stand in awe of their genius. Give bonus points for alliteration or rhyme or the most words per line or the best vocabulary. Students show that they really know a pattern when they can create an innovation on the basic pattern.

USE ANALOGIES OR OTHER MNEMONIC DEVICES TO HELP STUDENTS LEARN DIFFICULT-TO-REMEMBER GRAMMAR CONCEPTS.

When learners are faced with a problem that cannot be solved intuitively, they need to use a conscious strategy designed for clarifying the task. Because the brain can only conceptualize new things in terms of the things it already knows, you can use mnemonic devices and comparisons as a way of consciously assisting memory. People use rhymes, knuckle counting, and other gimmicks to remember the days in a month and other helpful information—devices that often make the information stick with learners for a lifetime.

Some of the best memory devices are those created by students. When you come to a difficult concept, such as using an irregular verb in the past tense, encourage students to create mnemonic devices: Ask students what the definition or concept they are trying to remember is like or could be compared to. You may be impressed by their answers. For example, students might compare an action verb to a play-by-play sportscast because the verb tells the action. If students have trouble coming up with a comparison that they can remember, brainstorm some examples with them, keeping in mind that we tend to remember colorful, moving, exaggerated, rhythmic, sensory, and humorous comparisons best. (For more background on the brain and language learning, see Chapter 12.)

MODEL THE CONCEPT...AND THEN MODEL SOME MORE!

If you find that the majority of students do not understand the grammar concept you've introduced, back up and model the concept for the whole group again, speaking aloud your thought process and asking them for help as you demonstrate the process (for example, how to tell an adjective from an adverb). You can further reinforce this process by having students redo the process in small groups with whole-group sharing at the end. The talk that is done in small groups helps students transfer the peer dialogue (spoken thought process) to internal thought processes. Pair discussions can

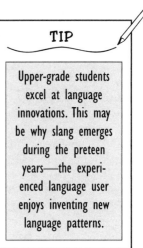

TIP

Upper-grade students excel at language innovations. This may be why slang emerges during the preteen years—the experienced language user enjoys inventing new language patterns.

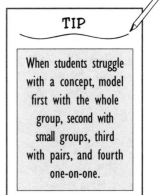

TIP

When students struggle with a concept, model first with the whole group, second with small groups, third with pairs, and fourth one-on-one.

work well for students who still cannot do the process alone. And finally, a few students may need individual coaching with you and experiences with materials at a more accessible level. Keeping this framework in mind when you plan can ensure that students have successful learning experiences.

WHEN THE WRITING IS WEAK, DO MORE PREWRITING.

The following lessons involve writing activities that engage students in using each grammar concept in a meaningful context. You can never do enough prewriting. Strategies such as brainstorming ideas, webbing details, sharing in pairs, freewriting, creating word banks, drawing, and role-playing will improve the quality of student writing. These strategies can be done at any time during the writing process, even at the very last minute. If students seem to be disengaged or unmotivated, try a quick prewriting activity to get everyone revved up for writing.

PLAN FOR LOTS OF SHARING.

Having students share their writing with peers while the writing is in process is crucial to their developing an understanding of language conventions and building a classroom community. Language is a social phenomenon; consequently, talking about ideas, drafts, and revisions with others helps students create the mental framework that later makes it possible to consciously revise the writing on the page. (For more background on social learning and language, see Chapter 12.)

Writing that isn't shared dies on the vine. The expectation of a significant audience outside the classroom changes the communication task in ways that can make students ask for more time and help in proofreading. You can find various audiences to whom students can show off their published writing; students from earlier grades, local senior citizens, and community members who have expertise with related topics or work in fields connected to writing can provide great reinforcement for students' efforts.

DON'T SKIP THE ART PART.

Writing assignments are too often passed down the row to the teacher without much notice or fanfare. In contrast, these lessons provide an art-based publishing opportunity for student writing that incorporates the targeted grammar concept. Artistic publishing can take writing to a higher level. Using color, texture, shapes, glitter, gel pens, fibers, stamps, pop-ups, or other special materials can ensure commitment from students and increase their sense of satisfaction upon completion of the project. I strive each term to make at least one writing project so special that it may be remembered as a lifetime literacy event.

TIP

Visuals can add a symbolic element that precedes writing; students have told me that they saw in their mind's eye how they wanted to publish their writing artistically before they had even begun writing.

ASSESS GRAMMAR CONCEPTS FROM STUDENTS' WRITING AND NOT FROM A STANDARDIZED TEST.

Traditional right-wrong questions about isolated sentences measure only those skills learned in the same format; such tests do not assess the ability to write well. An engaging and informative grammar assessment of the concepts taught in these lessons may be conducted in the form of a poetry performance rather than a mastery quiz. If students must pass a standardized test on usage, first make sure students understand how to use the concepts being tested in their own writing, then practice that particular test's format and discuss test-taking strategies. Remember that the larger educational goal is to teach students to choose to write for a lifetime, not just to pass a simplistic skills test created solely to gather statistics at one brief moment in time.

Questions I've Received From Teachers

HOW LONG DOES IT TAKE TO TEACH THESE LESSONS?

Depending on the language skills of your students and the length of your class periods, each chapter could take between two class periods and a week to complete. You may also pick and choose among the elements of a lesson to meet the needs of your students and your schedule.

FOR WHICH GRADE LEVELS IS THIS TYPE OF LESSON MOST APPROPRIATE?

I have used this lesson format with students in second grade through college. Second graders might grasp the pattern more than the grammar concepts, whereas college students appreciate reviewing these concepts in the context of writing. The collection of lessons in this book specifically targets grammar objectives that are taught in grades 5 and up.

WOULD THESE LESSONS WORK WITH ENGLISH LANGUAGE LEARNERS?

Yes. Teachers have told me that introducing the lessons with a poem and rereading it is a helpful entry into the language world for students who are just learning English, and that the poetry-writing frames and varied reinforcement activities offer them additional support.

WHY TEACH THESE SKILLS WITH POETRY RATHER THAN PROSE?

Poetry reinforces specific language structures by nature of its repeating patterns. Also, the brevity of the poems in this collection provides a quick writing experience for instruction. Moreover, poetry is playful, making grammar more palatable to students who have developed a distaste for it.

IS IT NECESSARY TO DO THE ONE-LINE MODELING PRIOR TO WRITING INDIVIDUAL POEMS?

I might skip this part with students who have a basic understanding of the grammar concept. However, having each student write one line of a class poem ensures that everyone can imitate the pattern before they work individually.

When is the Best Time to do the Grammar Mini-Lesson?

This one was hard for me to learn as a teacher. I was trained to do the mini-lesson first, at the beginning of the lesson. After learning more about theory and watching students have difficulty retaining the material, I tried moving the instructional moment inside of the writing activity. I have found that the longer you can wait, the better. Think of the poem as creating the need to learn the grammar. In the best of all worlds, I would want the students to ask me after they had completed their drafts, "Hey, what is this repeating line structure?"

Will Older Students Really Enjoy These Publication Projects?

I promise you that students will enjoy this much more than you think. If you are really in doubt about this, make it an extra-credit assignment or offer it to one student to try. I have taught inmates in prison, and believe it or not, when one student did a project for me, the other students were angry that I had not offered the project to all of them. Generally, students do their best writing when they know that they will publish it artistically. Another wonderful idea is to have older students give their project to younger students.

Can We Skip the Critical Thinking?

For a long time, this is the part that I skipped. What I found is that there is a big difference between my defining a concept and students' internalizing of it. Reflection is a slow process in which you must get students to explain the concept in their own language. Journaling or working in small groups increases the opportunity for everyone to reflect about the language feature. Too often, the teacher or those students who answer first are the only ones to consider why an activity is being done and what there is to learn from it.

Can Students Vary from the Original Format for Their Poems?

Absolutely! Creative variation is the final step of developmental mastery. It is only necessary that students include some repetition of the grammar element. Students often enjoy the challenge of including rhyme in their poems. Rhyme may cause students to create other grammar structures, which can become an excellent teachable moment for additional concepts.

Should We Mention the Other Repeating Grammar Elements in the Poems?

This depends on whether students have internalized the first grammar element. If they have, by all means, use the poem to explore other elements. Or wait until you are ready to work with the new grammar concept and then reintroduce the same poem—their familiarity with the poem will support their ability to analyze the new feature (and you only have to do minimal work introducing the poem). For example, Lansky's "Dumb and Dumber," the poem used for comparative adjectives, would be a good model for teaching the usage problem of when to punctuate *it's*.

How do skills learned in one context transfer to other writing assignments?

New skills often do not transfer from one context to another. With these grammar lessons, skill transfer is more likely since the context is a meaningful writing experience rather than a worksheet. That's why it's important to have students share their poems with a real audience rather than make these a dummy run, done for the teacher alone. A good idea is to require students to incorporate one or more of the grammar elements in their next writing assignment. For example, for bonus points, students could highlight one infinitive that they have added to an essay.

Can I use other model poems with these lessons?

Yes! When you start looking for grammar patterns in other poems, you will notice that structural repetition is a common poetic element. Even prose authors have a tendency to use some sentence patterns more than others. Students can help you discover and label more patterns. (Until I started teaching patterns from real texts, I never realized the obvious: grammar is everywhere! What a great concept to teach our developing writers.)

Challenging Assumptions About Language Learning

Language gives human beings the potential to imagine the future, create masterpieces, relate to other people, and change the world. Each language is made up of a set of complex, dynamic systems that are endlessly interesting to study. Regretfully, traditional grammar instruction overemphasizes drill work and simplistic definitions so that most students have developed an automatic "yuck" response to the mere mention of the word *grammar*.

The following cultural myths about grammar instruction reinforce antiquated practices, making it difficult for teachers to invent better teaching methodologies. However, once we've uncovered reliable information about language learning, we can develop new strategies for teaching students to use language effectively, which is the goal of this book.

✔ *Myth:*
   BEGINNING WRITERS MUST MASTER THE PARTS OF SPEECH BEFORE THEY LEARN TO WRITE.

Memorizing terms and identifying parts of speech in practice exercises are not the same thing as knowing how to generate sentences that employ educated language conventions. Teaching students to write well requires much more sophisticated learning than merely parroting definitions. Mastering terminology is a skill that is best learned in conjunction with learning how to do something rather than as a prerequisite that is separate from the activity. Spending large amounts of class time circling and labeling words in isolated sentences leaves little time for meaningful writing instruction.

✔ *Myth:*

GRAMMAR INSTRUCTION IMPROVES WRITING.

In more than 90 years of educational research there has never been a single study that demonstrates a direct correlation between skills-based grammar instruction and improved writing performance. The work of Constance Weaver (see Chapter 12) provides more information on these studies. In contrast, our cultural expectations—held by parents, administrators, teachers, and students alike—are that another dose of grammar drills will cure any and all writing problems. Teaching writing would be much easier if this assumption were true.

✔ *Myth:*

MOST CHILDREN DO NOT UNDERSTAND GRAMMAR.

Young children exhibit elaborate, intuitive knowledge about sentence structure, including usage rules such as forming plurals and conjugating verbs. Children learn language by imitating adults. Children's ability to understand the parts of speech has been demonstrated with nonsense words. When told to match the tool, substance, and action form of the nonsense words: "a sib," "some sib," and "sibbing," researchers found that 3-year-olds could identify the grammar forms successfully (Weaver, 1996). Everyone who can speak coherent sentences employs an understanding of language that far exceeds one's metacognitive awareness of these grammatical constructions. Students' intuitive understanding of language is a good starting point for school instruction.

Today I play, yesterday I played, tomorrow I will play...

Fact

WRITERS DO NEED GRAMMAR INSTRUCTION.

These misconceptions about grammar instruction do not mean that teachers should abandon the subject. Without grammar, our utterances would be little more than random groups of words. Grammar is a language system with predictable patterns. Patterns formulated as rules make us feel comfortable and safe in a world that is too often unpredictable. In fact, we actively create patterns in all areas of life: Sports statistics and even weather predictions are expressed with mathematical patterns; art and music are full of visual and sound patterns; and poetry and songs contain grammatical patterns.

The question then is not whether to teach grammar but which methods are the most effective. Instruction should match the brain's preferred cognitive-learning strategies. Imitation is the primary method that infants use to learn language. Babies imitate the patterns of facial expressions, gestures, sounds, words, and sentences without direct instruction. This knowledge can be called *intuitive* or *subconscious* because children do not know that they know it. The intuitive user can do the activity but cannot explain this knowledge explicitly or thoughtfully to someone else. One characteristic of learning by imitation is that at first the performance is more global or approximate. That is, the new learner imitates the most prominent features first and learns the smaller, more refined features last. This is why, for instance, educated adults are more concerned with the smaller features of language than children are. Tiny language errors such as misplaced modifiers can really irritate adults who are sophisticated language users, making it difficult for us to be patient with students' mistakes.

My process for teaching grammar is to move students from joyful, intuitive imitation to critical, conscious-level awareness of small language features during instruction and then to new, intuitive uses in everyday life. It can be difficult to introduce students to small linguistic features that run counter to their early language habits. Many of our language habits are dialect features that are part of our identities as members of families or communities that matter more to us than school or teachers. However, many people are masterful at the imitation of accents, dialects, and even the idiolects of well-known actors, politicians, and coworkers. It is possible to learn to speak and write in a different way if we have the motivation and the understanding to do so.

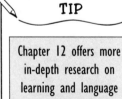

TIP

Chapter 12 offers more in-depth research on learning and language instruction that can support you in developing new writing- and reading-based strategies for teaching grammar.

Making the subconscious imitation of these patterns conscious can help students to gain better control of language. As they analyze imitated language patterns, students can become aware of what they know implicitly about grammar. Leading the class in metacognitive reflection about meaningful writing helps students recognize the grammar pattern on their own—I like to call these classroom discussions "wondering" about language. Thus, writing a poem, song, or rhyme comes first. Grammar is a teachable moment inside a larger lesson about writing something significant to share with others. Since language is acquired best during meaningful communication acts in real life, writing a dummy exercise that ends up in the trash provides a weak opportunity for language instruction. Artistic publishing and sharing with others can make writing more significant to the author. You'll find ideas for implementing these language-learning principles in each chapter, so you can target a key grammar objective while providing students with a meaningful, memorable language experience.

Hurray! Hurray! It's New Year's Day
by Kenn Nesbitt

Hurray! Hurray! It's New Year's Day!	1
The day we start anew.	2
So this year I've decided	3
to become a kangaroo.	4
Or maybe I will learn to fly,	5
or how to walk through walls,	6
or how to turn invisible,	7
or surf on waterfalls.	8
I'll make myself elastic,	9
and I'll teach myself to shrink.	10
I'll turn into a liquid,	11
and I'll pour me down the sink.	12
I'll visit other planets	13
and meet aliens galore.	14
I'll travel to the distant past	15
and ride a dinosaur.	16
I've got so many wondrous plans.	17
I'm starting right away.	18
Yes, this will be the best year yet.	19
Hurray! It's New Year's Day!	20

© 2007 by Kenn Nesbitt.

CHAPTER 2 COMPOUND SENTENCES

Holiday Poems

⌑ ⌑ ⌑ ⌑ ⌑ ⌑ **Instructional Objective** ⌑ ⌑ ⌑ ⌑ ⌑ ⌑ ⌑

Students write a "Holiday" poem that contains four compound sentences.

Source Poem: "Hurray! Hurray! It's New Year's Day" by Kenn Nesbitt (reproducible page 15)

Introductory Activity

Distribute copies of "Hurray! Hurray! It's New Year's Day" by Kenn Nesbitt. Read the poem once to the class. Assign students to underline or highlight the third stanza. Have students read the third stanza in unison as you read the other stanzas. Read the poem again, having students emphasize *I'll* by reading it louder than the rest of the text. Have the class repeat the reading aloud until all students are participating.

Modeling Activity

Imitate the model poem for a different, magical New Year's resolution. Assign each student to write two lines, each beginning with *I'll* and joined with *and*. Start by having students brainstorm a list of fantastic feats, such as inventing something or touring Egypt by camel. Select two of the ideas from the brainstorming list and model how to exaggerate or add hyperbole: *I'll invent a machine that can grade a set of student essays in thirty seconds, and I'll charge every teacher fifty dollars just to use it, and I'll visit King Tut's tomb, and I'll borrow some of his golden artifacts to decorate my room.* Point out that the two lines should have related ideas in order to be joined by "and." Have each student select a favorite feat from the class list and compose two related sentences joined by *and*.

TIP

The purpose of this activity is simply for students to imitate the compound sentence pattern found in the third stanza through an expressive reading; wait to discuss grammar terminology until after the imitation exercise is over and students are able to consciously imitate the pattern.

Conduct a read-aloud using the students' lines to create a class poem. Begin by reading the first two lines from Nesbitt's poem. Then have students take turns reading their lines. (Encourage each reader to revise any lines that are not complete, compound sentences so that the pattern stays consistent.) End by reading the last stanza from Nesbitt's poem. Repeat and have students suggest new ways to organize the lines so they sound best. Write the poem on chart paper. You might display it in the hallway or at a local greeting card store.

Grammar Mini-Lesson

Four ways to define compound sentences are listed below. Consider which explanations will help your particular students.

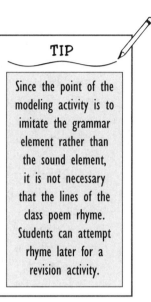

TIP

Since the point of the modeling activity is to imitate the grammar element rather than the sound element, it is not necessary that the lines of the class poem rhyme. Students can attempt rhyme later for a revision activity.

Function:
A compound sentence is two or more full sentences, punctuated as one. The two sentences are usually joined with a coordinating conjunction: *for, and, nor, but, or, yet, so.* A complete sentence, or an independent clause, contains at least a subject and a verb. A compound sentence joins two or more independent clauses.

I'll make myself elastic,   Compound sentence
and I'll teach myself to shrink.   with a *coordinating conjunction*

Meaning:
Compound sentences emphasize the close relationship between the ideas in the joined sentences. Beginning writers can use compound sentences to join sentences with a similar structure (notice that the sentences in Nesbitt's poem begin with the same subject and verb structure: *I'll make, I'll teach,* and so on). Advanced writers can use a semicolon to join compound sentences.

Identification:
The best way to spot a compound sentence is to look for a coordinating conjunction: *for, and, nor, but, or, yet, so.* (Helpful hint: The first letter of each of the coordinators join to spell FANBOYS.) Then, check to see that the conjunction is joining two full sentences rather than just parts of sentences. If the sentence contains two full sentences that are joined by a coordinating conjunction, it is a compound sentence.

Examples:
Have students identify the compound sentences in Nesbitt's poem. The third stanza contains two compound sentences: *I'll make myself elastic and*

TIP

Use an analogy to explain compound sentences. Compound sentences are like a set of twins. Twins are complete people alone, but they are related biologically to each other. Similarly, a compound sentence contains two sentences that are complete by themselves, but they share a similar relation.

I'll teach myself to shrink and *I'll turn into a liquid* and *I'll pour me down the sink.* The fourth stanza has two sentences with compound predicates, but without subjects these are not compound sentences. (You might ask students how they could make one of the lines into a compound sentence. For example, *I'll visit other planets / and meet aliens galore* becomes *I'll visit other planets / and I'll meet aliens galore.*)

Prewriting for an Individual Pattern Poem

Students can write their own "Holiday" poems for actions of their choice. With the class, brainstorm a list of traditional and nontraditional holidays: Independence Day, Halloween, Valentine's Day, Mother's Day, April Fool's Day, Father's Day, the first day of baseball season, Groundhog Day, and National Catfish Day. Have each student select a favorite holiday. Direct students to jot down as many ideas as they can about their holiday, such as typical activities, foods, traditions, presents, and decorations. Tell students to exaggerate their ideas to make their poems more interesting.

Writing the Poem

Have students draft their own poems, imitating the compound sentence pattern of the original model. Use the frame on page 20 as a guide.

Publishing Activity: Tumbling Book

* Begin with two square sheets of paper. Fold each sheet in half and cut or tear along the folds to make four rectangular strips.

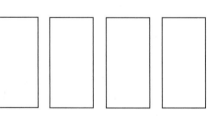

* Turn these four strips lengthwise. Fold each in half lightly to determine the center line, and then fold the sides in to this center, creasing the two folds both forward and backward for flexibility. This will look like a cabinet with double doors. Repeat for all four strips.

TIP

Have students make a practice book out of copy paper first before using heavier card stock for the final copy. Discarded file folders can be used for card stock.

- Unfold the strips. Place two strips side by side horizontally. Next, place the two other strips on top of the others vertically (bottom and top strips should be positioned in the opposite direction).

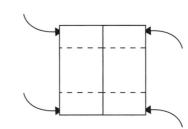

- Glue the four outer corners of the strips together. (Only glue the outer corners, not the whole strip.)

- Open the book carefully from the center and re-crease the folds. Repeat two more times, re-creasing the folds. Remember that the book always opens from the center.

- The book opens sequentially to reveal four differently shaped pages (see below). On side 1, decorate a cover with an image that represents the poem (you might punch small holes in each half of the cover to insert brass brads as doorknobs, as shown in the photo); on side 2, write the poem; on side 3, write the title or an inspirational line; and on side 4, write the author's name.

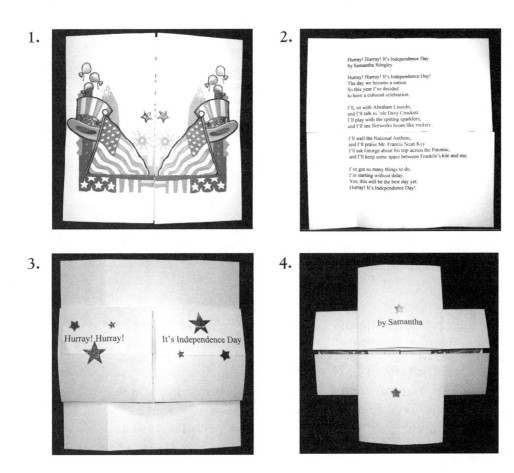

1.

2.

3.

4.

❖ ❖

Poem Frame

Hurray! Hurray! It's _____ Day!	1
(holiday)	
The day we start anew.	2
So this year I've decided	3
to _____.	4
(activity)	
I'll _____,	5
(activity)	
and I'll _____.	6
(activity)	
I'll _____,	7
(activity)	
and I'll _____.	8
(activity)	
I'll _____,	9
(activity)	
and I'll _____.	10
(activity)	
I'll _____,	11
(activity)	
and I'll _____.	12
(activity)	
I've got so many wondrous plans.	13
I'm starting right away.	14
Yes, this will be the best year yet.	15
Hurray! It's _____ Day!	16
(holiday)	

TIP

The second and fourth stanzas have been omitted and the third stanza has been repeated to emphasize compound sentences.

Critical-Thinking Time

These thought teasers are provided for your students to discuss in small groups and then share with the whole class for further wondering and discussion.

• The third stanza of Nesbitt's poem is made of two compound sentences, but stanza four does not have any compound sentences. Explain what one thing is different about the sentence structures in stanza four. Tell why they are not compound sentences and explain what type of sentences they are. (*Stanza four does not have an* I'll *in the sentences after the* and. *There is only one subject in each sentence. These sentences have compound predicates but are not compound sentences.*)

• Authors choose to combine two sentences into one compound sentence because the two sentences have a closely related meaning. Examine the compound sentences in stanza three and explain how the meaning is related in each of the compound sentences. (*The first sentence tells a form that he will adopt and the second sentence tells what action will be done when the speaker takes on that form.*)

• Nesbitt uses only one conjunction: *and*. Rewrite the fourth stanza, converting the sentences into compound sentences, using different coordinating conjunctions: *for, nor, but, or, yet, so*. You may add new details. (*A possible answer: I'll visit other planets, but I won't forget to bring along some oxygen from Earth.*)

Grammar Reinforcement Activity

Use the following activity to reinforce the basic structure of compound sentences and provide an opportunity to discuss additional information or confusing features.

Divide the class into two groups to play a compound sentence matching game. Have one student from each team write a simple sentence on the board, followed by a comma and the conjunction *and*. The second team has two minutes for their members to write related "matching" sentences that could complete the compound sentence. The second team scores one point for every matching sentence. The other team can protest any sentence that is not complete or is not related in meaning. For variety, require that teams use different coordinating conjunctions. Repeat for several rounds; the team with the most points wins.

Grammar Extension Activity

An additional concept about compound sentences can be introduced to students who want to learn more, or this activity can be used for an extra-credit assignment.

Punctuating Compound Sentences:

When a coordinating conjunction such as *and* joins two sentences, it usually is preceded by a comma. This is important since conjunctions such as *and* can be used to join words as well as sentences. The comma signals to the reader that the conjunction is separating sentences rather than words. Note the difference in the sentences below:

I went to the store to buy salt and pepper.
I went to the store to buy salt, and pepper was on sale.

If the two sentences that are joined are not confusing and they are brief, the comma can be left out, but the comma is correct for joining sentences with a coordinating conjunction. Ask students to consider why Nesbitt chose to leave out the comma in compound sentences in the third stanza. No commas are necessary if the conjunction is used to join parts of a sentence. In the fourth stanza of Nesbitt's poem the *and* is joining two predicates or two verbs rather than two full sentences.

A compound sentence can also be joined with a semicolon. A semicolon is used when the second sentence restates or further expands the first one. Challenge students to write a stanza for their poem using a semicolon.

I've decided to become a kangaroo; I will enjoy jumping instead of walking.

Topic Variations

You can change the assignment to include different types of celebrations. Students can write "Holiday" poems about the following:

- a newly created holiday such as Pet Day or Skateboard Day.

- a birthday celebration for a historical person such as Amelia Earhart or Dan Rice.

- a Founders Day designed for your school district, neighborhood, or town.

Writing About Literature

Students can compose "Holiday" poems based on an event in a novel, such as

- for *Whirligig*, "Forgiveness Day" started by Lea's mother.

- for *The Giver*, "Assignment Day" for the twelves.

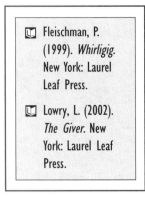

Fleischman, P. (1999). *Whirligig*. New York: Laurel Leaf Press.

Lowry, L. (2002). *The Giver*. New York: Laurel Leaf Press.

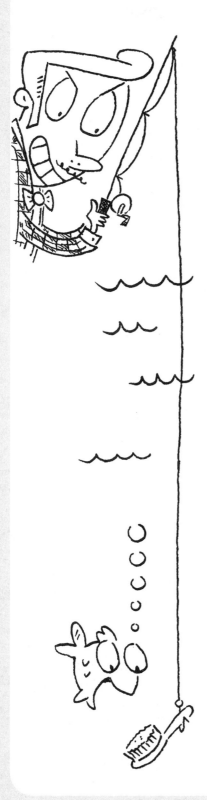

Archie B. McCall
by Jack Prelutsky

The shrewdest salesman anywhere	1
is Archie B. McCall,	2
he's king of selling anything	3
to anyone at all,	4
Archie's ways are so persuasive	5
he's been never known to fail,	6
he has sold a yak a jacket,	7
sacks of feathers to a snail.	8
He has sold a fish a hairbrush,	9
and a snake a pair of shoes,	10
peddled Pogo sticks and purses	11
to a troop of kangaroos,	12
he has sold a camel earmuffs,	13
and a trumpet to a moose,	14
a bikini to a beaver,	15
an umbrella to a goose.	16
No one ever turns down Archie,	17
for when Archie's at his best,	18
he can sell an eagle glasses,	19
he can sell a worm a vest,	20
Archie's simply irresistible,	21
he's matchless, he's a whiz,	22
he talked me into buying this—	23
I wonder what it is.	24

© 1984 by Jack Prelutsky.

Best Seller Poems

¤ ¤ ¤ ¤ ¤ ¤ **Instructional Objective** ¤ ¤ ¤ ¤ ¤ ¤ ¤

Students write a "Best Seller" poem that contains 12 direct objects and 11 indirect objects.

Source Poem: "Archie B. McCall" by Jack Prelutsky (reproducible page 23)

Introductory Activity

Distribute copies of "Archie B. McCall" by Jack Prelutsky and read aloud the poem once. Ask students to underline or highlight all the words that name things that Archie B. McCall sold and circle all the animals to which he sold the items. Select two volunteers who have marked all the sold items and animals. (Make sure to check that they've underlined and circled the right words—see the Grammar Mini-Lesson for answers.) Assign one student to read aloud the names of the sold items and the other to read aloud the names of the animals as you read the rest of the poem. Now read aloud the poem again, this time with each student volunteer leading one side of the classroom in reading the names of the sold items or animals.

Modeling Activity

Imitate the model poem for different objects and animals. Assign each student to write one line, following this pattern: "He has sold a ____ to a ____." Start by having students brainstorm a list of several animals, including mammals, reptiles, and insects. Have each student select a favorite animal from the class list to put in the second blank. Tell students to fill in the first blank with an unusual object. For fun, ask students to use alliteration for the object and the animal.

TIP

Since the point of the modeling activity is to imitate the grammar element rather than the sound element, it is not necessary that the lines of the class poem rhyme. Students can attempt rhyme later for a revision activity.

Share everyone's lines by reading them aloud. Begin by reading the first six lines from Prelutsky's poem. Have students take turns reading their lines, and have peers help them fix any lines that do not include a sold item and an animal. End by reading the last four lines from Prelutsky's poem. The class poem could be displayed at a local car dealership.

Grammar Mini-Lesson

Four ways to define direct and indirect objects are listed below. Consider which explanations will help your particular students.

Function:
A direct object is a noun or pronoun following an action verb that identifies who or what receives the action of the verb. Not every sentence has a direct object, but the subject-verb–direct object pattern is very common in English.

In order for an indirect object to appear in a sentence, there must also be a direct object. An indirect object is a noun or pronoun following an action verb and identifies *to* whom or *for* whom the action of the verb is done and who is receiving the direct object.

He has sold a fish a *hairbrush*.   *direct object*
He has sold a *fish* a hairbrush.   *indirect object*

Sentences can have more than one direct or indirect object.

He has sold a fish a *hairbrush* and a snake a *pair of shoes*.   *direct objects*
He has sold a *fish* a hairbrush and a *snake* a pair of shoes.   *indirect objects*

Meaning:
Direct objects are used to discuss what has changed or been affected by the action, and indirect objects are used to explain for whom the change was done. Beginning writers can use this basic sentence structure to express ideas.

Identification:
Direct objects are nouns or pronouns that follow the verb and answer the question of who or what receives the action. Indirect objects are nouns or pronouns that follow the verb and either begin with the preposition *to* or *for* (or the preposition is not stated but understood). Generally, indirect objects can be dropped out and the sentence will still make sense. If the element is a noun or a pronoun following a verb, it is a direct object. If the element answers "who or what receives the action?" and it does or could begin with *to* or *for*, it is an indirect object.

TIP

Use a postal analogy to explain direct and indirect objects. A direct object is like a package being mailed to someone. An indirect object is the person to whom the letter is addressed.

Example:

Have students identify the direct and indirect objects in Prelutsky's poem. Direct objects: *jacket, sacks of feathers, hairbrush, pair of shoes, sticks and purses, earmuffs, trumpet, bikini, umbrella, me, glasses, vest* and *this.* Indirect objects: *yak, snail, fish, snake, troop of kangaroos, camel, moose, beaver, goose, eagle,* and *worm.*

Prewriting for an Individual Pattern Poem

Students can write their own "Best Seller" poems for objects of their choice. Ask students to write on a piece of paper the name of a friend or character they know who's very convincing: this is someone who could serve as the salesperson in their poem. Then as a class brainstorm a list of types of people who might be customers, such as laborers, professionals, artists, athletes, hobbyists, tradespeople, trainers, and scientists. Have students each select 11 types of customers and list one or two unusual objects that could be sold to each one.

Writing the Poem

Have students draft their own poems, imitating the repeating "s/he has sold" pattern of the original model. Use the frame on page 27 as a guide.

Publishing Activity: Wallet Book

TIP

Download images of ID's and money to print and cut out to add to the wallet. Slits can be cut on the backside of the envelope to hold ID's and photographs.

- Start with a business-sized envelope. (Colored envelopes look more realistic. White envelopes can be dyed brown by brushing lightly with strong coffee or tea.)

- Tuck in the flap and outline the edges of the envelope with a black pen.

- Fold the envelope in half vertically and decorate the cover with favorite designs or initials.

- Print out the poem onto regular paper and cut it down to 4 inches in width. Insert the poem into the top of the envelope.

Poem Frame

The shrewdest salesperson anywhere   1

is _____,   2
     (salesperson's name)

s/he's queen/king of selling anything   3

to anyone at all,   4

_____'s ways are so persuasive   5
(first name)

s/he's been never known to fail,   6

s/he has sold a _____ to a _____,   7
         (object)   (person)

a _____ to a _____.   8
   (object)   (person)

S/He has sold a _____ to a _____,   9
         (object)   (person)

and a _____ to a _____,   10
      (person)   (object)

peddled _____ and _____ to a _____,   11
     (objects)   (objects)   (person)

s/he has sold a _____ to a _____,   12
         (object)   (person)

and a _____ to a _____,   13
    (object)   (person)

a _____ to a _____,   14
   (object)   (person)

a _____ to a _____.   15
   (object)   (person)

No one ever turns down _____,   16
          (first name)

for when _____'s at her/his best,   17
     (first name)

s/he can sell a _____ to a _____,   18
        (object)   (person)

s/he can sell a _____ to a _____,   19
        (object)   (person)

_____'s simply irresistible,   20
(first name)

s/he's matchless, s/he's a whiz,   21

s/he talked me into buying this—   22

I wonder what it is.   23

> **TIP**
>
> For consistency, all of the indirect objects have been changed. They are now preceded by *to*.

Critical-Thinking Time

The thought teasers are provided for your students to discuss in small groups and then share with the whole class for further wondering and discussion.

- Sentences that have indirect objects almost always have direct objects. Check Prelutsky's poem to see how many direct and indirect object pairs have the direct object listed first. Explain how this structure is different from the pairs in which the indirect object comes last. (*Five pairs have the direct object first, and six pairs have the indirect object first. In the pairs in which the indirect object comes last, Prelutsky uses* to *in front of the indirect object to avoid confusion.*)

- Pronouns such as *me, you, him, her,* and *them* can be either direct or indirect objects. Find the line in which Prelutsky used *me* and determine if it is used as a direct or indirect object. Compose two sentences, using *her* as a direct object in one sentence and as an indirect object in the other. (*The line is:* he talked me into buying this. Me *is the direct object. Possible answer; Direct object: He convinced her. Indirect object: He gave her his number.*)

- Write a letter from Bart Simpson to Santa asking for a specific present for each member of his family. (*A possible answer: Santa, please give my dad a million doughnuts.*)

Grammar Reinforcement Activity

Use the following activity to reinforce what students have learned about objects in a sentence and provide an opportunity to discuss additional information or confusing features.

Divide the class into groups to create holiday gift lists for famous people. Let each group create a five-item gift list for a favorite celebrity or character from a book. Have students write sentences using both a direct and an indirect object for each item. For example: *I will give Jim Carrey a clownfish.* Share lists with the whole class. For fun, students can create a series of gifts with the same theme, such as humor or vanity.

Grammar Extension Activity

An additional concept about direct and indirect objects can be introduced to students who want to learn more, or this activity can be used for an extra-credit assignment.

Passive Voice:

When the receiver of the action is moved to the subject of the sentence, the sentence is less active and more passive. Passive-voice sentences reverse the subject and direct object. Usually, these constructions sound awkward because the actor is placed after the action. In most writing, the active voice is preferred.

Active Voice   He has sold a yak a jacket.
Passive Voice   A jacket was sold to a yak by him.

Challenge students to find passive-voice sentences in a local news story and rewrite them in the active voice. For example: ~~The store was robbed by an unarmed octogenarian~~. *The unarmed octogenarian robbed the store.*

Topic Variations

You can change the assignment to be about a different activity. Students can write "Best Seller" poems for:

- a famous performer who has sung or played various songs for many types of people.

- a famous magician who has performed various tricks for many types of audiences.

- a philanthropist who has given resources to many needy groups.

Writing About Literature

Students can compose "Best Seller" poems that describe the talents or skills of a literary character. For example:

- the problems Blue Avenger solves in *The Adventures of Blue Avenger*.

- the items Dicey gets for her brothers and sister in *Dicey's Song*.

📖 Howe, N. (2000). *The Adventures of Blue Avenger.* New York: Harper.

📖 Voigt, C. (2003). *Dicey's Song.* New York: Aladdin

I Am Wunk
by Jack Prelutsky

I am Wunk, a wacky wizard,   1

and I wield a willow wand.   2

I wave it once, and there you swim,   3

a minnow in a pond,   4

I wave it twice, and there you sit,   5

a lizard on a log.   6

I wave it thrice, and there you fly,   7

a fly before a frog.   8

I am Wunk, a wily wizard,   9

and I hold a crystal sphere.   10

I spin it with my fingers,   11

you've a carrot in your ear.   12

I roll it on the table,   13

you've an anvil on your head.   14

I place it on your pillow,   15

you've a lion in your bed.   16

I am Wunk, a wondrous wizard,   17

and I wear a woolen hat.   18

I take it off and fold it,   19

you are smaller than a cat.   20

I put it in my pocket,   21

you are smaller than a mouse.   22

Do be quick, your doorbell's ringing . . .   23

I am Wunk outside your house.   24

© 1990 by Jack Prelutsky.

Teaching Grammar With Perfect Poems for Middle School • Scholastic Teaching Resources

Medieval Poems

☒ ☒ ☒ ☒ ☒ ☒ **Instructional Objective** ☒ ☒ ☒ ☒ ☒ ☒

Students write a "Medieval" poem that contains three appositives.

Source Poem: "I Am Wunk" by Jack Prelutsky (reproducible page 30)

Introductory Activity

Distribute copies of "I Am Wunk" by Jack Prelutsky. Read the poem once to the class. Have students underline or highlight all the "wizard phrases" that follow the word *Wunk* in the first line of each stanza. Ask students to select whether they would rather be a "wacky," "wily," or "wondrous" wizard and instruct them to read the chosen wizard phrase in unison as you read the rest of the lines.

Modeling Activity

Imitate the model poem, substituting different descriptions for wizard. Start by having students select a name and three alliterative descriptions. For example: *I am Olivia, an outlandishly outrageous wizard, and I wear opaque eyewear.* Assign students to write one sentence following this pattern: "I am _____, a _____ wizard, and I wear _____." You may wish to have them use dictionaries or thesauruses to fill in the blanks with one or more alliterative words.

Organize a reading of the class poem by having students volunteer their lines in alphabetical order by their wizard's name. Add two culminating last lines such as: *Do be nice to me, dear, Or I will make you disappear.* You could display the class poem with fantasy books at the local library.

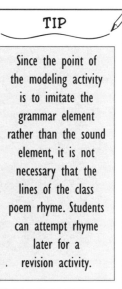

TIP

Since the point of the modeling activity is to imitate the grammar element rather than the sound element, it is not necessary that the lines of the class poem rhyme. Students can attempt rhyme later for a revision activity.

⬧ ⬧

Grammar Mini-Lesson

Four ways to define appositives are listed below. Consider which explanations will help your particular students.

Function:
An appositive is a word, phrase, or clause that follows a noun or pronoun and is equal to it. An appositive is another noun that renames the noun directly in front of it. An appositive follows a noun.

He told about the wizard, *Wunk*.	word
He told about Wunk, *a wacky wizard*.	phrase
He told about Wunk, *who has been a wizard for many years*.	clause

Meaning:
An appositive adds clarification to the noun or name that precedes it. Beginning writers can use appositives to combine two short sentences into one.

Identification:
The best way to test for an appositive is to drop it and see if the sentence still makes sense without it. Next, check to see if it follows a noun and renames it. If the element can be dropped and it follows and renames a noun, it is an appositive.

He told about the wizard, ~~Wunk~~.   The appositive can be dropped.

Example:
Have students identify the appositives in Prelutsky's poem: *a wacky wizard, a wily wizard*, and *a wondrous wizard*.

Prewriting for an Individual Pattern Poem

Students can write their own "Medieval" poems for other medieval or fantasy roles such as king, queen, jester, knight, dragon, peasant, page, princess, prince, servant, or minstrel. After students select a role, have them create an alliterative name and three descriptions that can serve as appositives. Have students also create a list of actions that complement each of the three descriptive traits.

Writing the Poem

Have students draft their own poems, imitating the repeating "I am" pattern of the original model. Use the frame on page 33 as a guide.

TIP

Use an analogy to explain appositives. An appositive is like a mirror held up to the noun or pronoun in front of it. An appositive reflects the meaning of the noun or pronoun.

❖ ❖

Poem Frame

I am _____, a _____ _____,   1
     (name)   (first description)   (role)

and I _____.   2
    (action related to the trait)

I _____.   3
  (action related to the trait)

I _____.   4
  (action related to the trait)

I _____.   5
  (action related to the trait)

I am _____, a _____ _____,   6
     (name)   (second description) (role)

and I _____.   7
    (action related to the trait)

I _____.   8
  (action related to the trait)

I _____.   9
  (action related to the trait)

I _____.   10
  (action related to the trait)

I am _____, a _____ _____,   11
     (name)   (third description)   (role)

and I _____.   12
    (action related to the trait)

I _____.   13
  (action related to the trait)

I _____.   14
  (action related to the trait)

Do be nice to me, dear,   15

Or I will _____.   16
    (action)

TIP

The stanzas have been simplified to emphasize the appositives in the first line.

Publishing Activity: Character Card

• On neutral card stock, draw a face (or print one from an Internet download) that matches the poem's main character (e.g., a Santa face for a wizard).

33

• Draw two arms on neutral card stock and two shoes, sleeves, and a hat for the character on colored card stock. Cut out the face, arms, sleeves, hat, and shoes, and color or decorate them. Glue sleeves onto the arms.

• Cut out a 5- by 8-inch rectangle from colored card stock or filing cards. Punch a hole at the two top corners of the rectangle and at the top of each arm. Attach with brass brads.

• Glue on the face, hat, and shoes. Cut out a 10- by 8-inch rectangle from white card stock and fold it in half on the 10-inch side to make a 5- by 8-inch card. Glue the front of the card to the back of the character's body (the rectangles should match up). Write the poem on the inside of the card or print out the poem, trim the paper to size, and glue it to the inside of the card.

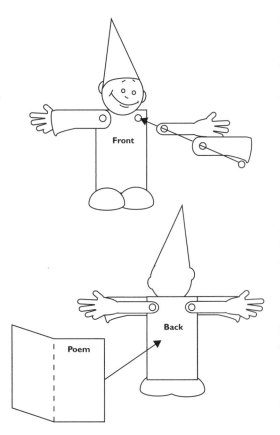

TIP

Embellish the character's hat with stickers. Make accessories from craft or recycled items— a plastic straw topped with a star sticker might serve as a wand for a wizard, for instance.

I Am a Wizard
By Christy Roy

I am Andrew, an aggressively aggravated wizard,
and I wear an awful frown.

I am Brandy, a breathtakingly beautiful wizard,
and I wear a beaded gown.

I am Carla, a continuously conniving wizard,
and I wear a cunning smirk.

I am Dan, a dashingly debonair wizard,
and I wear a double breasted suit.

I am Enrique, an easily excitable wizard,
and I wear enormous earrings.

I am Fred, a frighteningly ferocious wizard,
and I wear a fringe of spikes.

I am Gertrude, a graciously giving wizard,
and I wear a good-natured smile.

I am Herbert, a humongous hungry wizard,
and I wear huge hand-me-downs.

I am Lisa, a lively leaping wizard,
and I wear a lavender leotard.

I am Mary, a monstrously mean wizard,
and I wear a menacing scowl.

I am Olivia, an outlandishly outrageous wizard,
and I wear opaque eyewear.

Do be nice to us, my dear,
Or we will make you disappear

☒ ☒

Critical-Thinking Time

The thought teasers are provided for your students to discuss in small groups and then share with the whole class for further wondering and discussion.

• An appositive is a noun, pronoun, or noun phrase following and renaming or explaining another. In the poem, all the noun phrases define the name *Wunk*. Write a new sentence in which *Wunk* is the appositive. (*A possible answer: The wondrous wizard, Wunk, is wearing a woolen hat.*)

• Appositives should be placed directly following the noun phrase. In these lines from the poem the sentence structure is inverted: *There you swim, a minnow in a pond.* Rephrased, the sentence would be: *You swim there, a minnow in a pond.* Rewrite the sentence, placing the appositive in the correct position. (*You, a minnow in a pond, swim there.*) Discuss why the poet chose the inverted structure for the poem.

• Write an introduction for a famous media star that your grandparent might not know, using an appositive. Start with: *Grandpa, I'd like you to meet . . .* (*A possible answer: Grandpa, I'd like you to meet Ice Cube, a famous rapper and actor.*)

Grammar Reinforcement Activity

Use the following activity to reinforce the function of appositives and provide an opportunity to discuss additional information or confusing features.

To prepare for a game of Nursery Rhyme Appositives, copy onto cards the first sentence from common nursery rhymes (prepare at least 12 cards). Divide the class into small groups and distribute one card to each group. Students are to rewrite the sentences, adding an appositive after every noun. For example: *Jack, a nice boy, and Jill, his clumsy sister, went up the hill, a large pile of dirt, to fetch a pail, a metal bucket, of water, H_2O.* Share each group's answers, keeping track of the number of appositives used correctly. The group with the most appositives wins one point. Repeat for several rounds; the group with the most points wins.

Grammar Extension Activity

An additional concept about appositives can be introduced to students who want to learn more, or this activity can be used for an extra-credit assignment.

When to Use Commas With an Appositive:
Appositives follow a noun or pronoun and often take commas before and after, because they usually provide nonessential information.

comma   I am Wunk, a wacky wizard.
commas   Wunk, a wacky wizard, wears a woolen hat.

However, it is possible for appositives to provide essential information that is needed to keep the main clause from being confusing.

no comma   I cannot find the wizard Wunk.

In this case only *Wunk* is needed. The appositive does not need to be set off by commas since it doesn't just modify *wizard*—it specifies one of many wizards. Nonrestrictive appositives that take commas are more common than restrictive appositives that do not. Challenge students to find appositives in their science or history textbooks and to write an explanation for the punctuation of each sentence.

Topic Variations

You can change the assignment to be about a different role. Students can write "Medieval" poems for:

- a career of interest.

- a position in a team sport or individual Olympic event.

- an American president.

Writing About Literature

Students can compose "Medieval" poems about a literary character, including

- any wizard from *Harry Potter and the Sorcerer's Stone*.

- Le Jardiniere, the jester, in *Queen's Own Fool*.

Rowling, J. K. (1999). *Harry Potter and the Sorcerer's Stone*. New York: Scholastic.

Yolen, J., & Harris, R. (2001). *Queen's Own Fool*. New York: Putnam.

I Remember
by Jana Turner

I remember watching my older sister's fingers breeze across the piano keys   1
as I sat next to her on the sturdy bench.

I remember waiting anxiously in my mother's car   2
for my first lesson with Uncle Frank.

I remember practicing diligently   3
while my friends were playing outside or watching television.

I remember memorizing "Miracle Melody" for my first recital   4
when I was eleven years old.

I remember wondering if I would ever be able   5
to play any pieces by Beethoven or Bach.

I remember playing for the first time in front   6
of an audience full of strangers.

I remember seeing the look on my faithful father's face   7
when I won first place at my final recital.

I remember feeling peaceful and proud   8
when I began to create my own colorful music.

Some things I may forget, but when it comes to piano,   9
there are many things that I remember.

© 2005 by Jana Turner.

Teaching Grammar With Perfect Poems for Middle School • Scholastic Teaching Resources

CHAPTER 5 **GERUNDS**

I Remember Poems

⊠ ⊠ ⊠ ⊠ ⊠ ⊠ **Instructional Objective** ⊠ ⊠ ⊠ ⊠ ⊠ ⊠

Students write an "I Remember" poem that contains eight gerunds.

Source Poem: "I Remember" by Jana Turner (reproducible page 37)

Introductory Activity

Distribute copies of "I Remember" by Jana Turner. Read the poem aloud to the class. Assign students to underline or highlight all the *-ing* words following the word *remember* in the poem. Have students read the *-ing* words in unison as you read the rest of the lines. Then have students read the poem again, with the class beginning each line in a chorus of "I remember" and with volunteers reading solo, from the *-ing* word to the end of the line.

Modeling Activity

Imitate the model poem for a new memory about some experience the students have in common, such as being in kindergarten, playing dodgeball at recess, or attending a community festival. This memory will be the topic of the class poem. To prepare students to write a line about the memory, have them brainstorm a list of remembered events or experiences, such as wearing new shoes to school or wondering whether they would make new friends in kindergarten. Select one or more of the ideas from the brainstorming list and model how to begin the phrase with an *-ing* word. You may also wish to model replacing verbs such as *having* or *being* with more vivid ones. For example, *I remember stumbling on the stairs in my newly purchased shoes* is much stronger than *I remember having trouble on the stairs in my newly purchased shoes*. Have each student select a favorite item from the class list and compose one line.

Create the class poem by having students volunteer their lines in a time sequence. Ask for an event that happened first, next, and so on. Accept volunteered lines, helping students revise to match the model structure as you record the lines on the board or overhead. When you have eight lines, add Turner's last line, replacing *piano* with the new topic. The class poem could be published in the school newsletter, the yearbook, or a local paper.

Grammar Mini-Lesson

Four ways to define gerunds, the *-ing* words in Turner's poem, are listed below. Consider which explanations will help your particular students.

Function:
A gerund is a verb with an *-ing* ending that acts as a noun. Gerunds belong to the category of verbals, which are verbs that can function as another part of speech. A gerund can occupy the subject or object position in a sentence. It can also be the object of the prepositional phrase or predicate nominative.

Practicing is hard work.	gerund as subject
I hate *practicing*.	gerund as direct object
He is bad at *practicing*.	gerund as object of a prepositional phrase
My least favorite activity is *practicing*.	gerund as predicate nominative

A gerund phrase contains the gerund plus any extra modifying words.

I remember *practicing diligently*.	gerund phrase

Meaning:
Gerunds provide a way to speak about actions as topics. Because they are made from verbs, gerunds are more lively than regular nouns. Advanced writers can use gerund phrases for sentence variety and to further describe and qualify the action being discussed.

Identification:
A gerund always ends with *-ing* without exception. Since gerunds are verbs acting as nouns, you can test any verb ending in *-ing* by substituting the word with the pronoun "it": If the *-ing* word can be replaced with *it*, you have a gerund.

[*It*] is hard work.	*Practicing* is a gerund.
I hate [*it*].	*Practicing* is a gerund.
He is bad at [*it*].	*Practicing* is a gerund.
My least favorite activity is [*it*].	*Practicing* is a gerund.
He is practicing.	*Practicing* is not a gerund.

⊠ ⊠

TIP

Use an insect analogy to explain gerunds. Gerunds are like butterflies. Caterpillars grow **wing**s in order to change into butterflies. Likewise, gerunds are verbs with *-ing* that change into nouns. (Jana Turner)

Example:
Have students identify the gerunds in Turner's poem: *watching, waiting, practicing, memorizing, wondering, playing, seeing,* and *feeling. Playing* is a verb within a subordinate clause.

Prewriting for an Individual Pattern Poem

Students can write their own "I Remember" poems for several memorable events. Have students each create a graph of life events. Distribute graph paper or rulers. Have students mark the years of their lives on the horizontal axis and the numerals 1 to 5 above and below the vertical axis to rank their experiences as positive or negative. Have students place a dot and label it for eight or more life events, such as trips, accidents, family changes, best birthdays, friendships, new skills, and pets. The dots can be connected to create a graph.

Writing the Poem

Have students draft their own poems, imitating the repeating "I remember" pattern of the original model. Use the frame below as a guide.

Poem Frame

I remember _____ _____.   1
          (action + i*ng*)   (specific details)

I remember _____ _____.   2
          (action + i*ng*)   (specific details)

I remember _____ _____.   3
          (action + i*ng*)   (specific details)

I remember _____ _____.   4
          (action + i*ng*)   (specific details)

I remember _____ _____.   5
          (action + i*ng*)   (specific details)

I remember _____ _____.   6
          (action + i*ng*)   (specific details)

I remember _____ _____.   7
          (action + i*ng*)   (specific details)

I remember _____ _____.   8
          (action + i*ng*)   (specific details)

Some things I may forget, but when it comes to my life,   9
there are many things that I remember.

Publishing Activity: Faux Leather Journal

- Cut a large rectangle out of the front of a paper grocery bag.

- Crumple the paper several times to create wrinkles. Unfold, leaving in the wrinkles. Rub dark shoe polish, ink, or crayons over one side to create a leathery look.

- Cut the paper in half, making two sheets approximately 11 by 5 inches. (Only one sheet is needed to make a journal cover, so students may share.)

- Cut out a sheet of cardboard slightly smaller than the paper (the back of a pad of paper, a cereal box, or mailing envelope can be used). Fold the cardboard in half and crease it flat.

- Set the cardboard in the center of the paper with the stained side down. Fold over all four edges of the paper and glue to the cardboard (this is the inside cover of the book).

- Fold a sheet of copy paper in half to make a booklet and trim it to fit inside the journal. Write the poem on the inside right-hand side of the page. Fasten the folded paper in the book with an elastic band or yarn (this should encircle the binding).

- Embellish with a paper title plate, corners, a keyhole, and key.

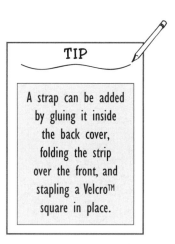

TIP

A strap can be added by gluing it inside the back cover, folding the strip over the front, and stapling a Velcro™ square in place.

Critical-Thinking Time

The thought teasers are provided for your students to discuss in small groups and then share with the whole class for further wondering and discussion.

* Gerunds are useful for sentence variety, especially gerund phrases, which can include lots of extra information. For Turner's poem, determine which line contains the most information. (*The first line has the greatest number of words and explains who, what, when, where, and how.*)

* Some of Turner's sentences have direct objects after the gerund and some do not. Find three lines that have direct objects following the gerund. Find the sentences that have adverbs after the gerunds. (*The first, fourth, and seventh lines have direct objects following the gerunds. The second and third lines have adverbs following the gerunds.*)

* Write a title for a *Sports Illustrated* article that contains a gerund. (*Possible answers: Tiger Woods Is Tops in Golfing. Hitting Home Runs Is Rodriguez's Goal.*)

Grammar Reinforcement Activity

Use the following activity to reinforce students' understanding of gerunds and provide an opportunity to discuss additional information or confusing features.

Make a set of six to eight cards that name current celebrity favorites of the class as well as cartoon characters that students know well. Divide the class into two groups to play Celebrity What's My Line. Have teams each draw a celebrity card and compose five "I remember" sentences (with gerunds) that describe memories of their famous person or character. Next, have a student on each team read the "I remember" sentences to the other team. The object is for the listening team to name the celebrity whom the statements describe. Any team that reads a sentence without a gerund automatically loses that round. Repeat for several rounds; the team with the most correct answers wins.

Grammar Extension Activity

An additional concept about gerunds can be introduced to students who want to learn more, or this activity can be used for an extra-credit assignment.

Gerund Placement:
Gerunds can be placed anywhere a noun can be placed in a sentence.
Gerunds can be placed in the following positions:

subject	*Playing* piano is my hobby.
direct object	I remember *playing* piano.
object of the preposition	I am good at *playing* piano.
predicate nominative	My favorite hobby is *playing* piano.

Challenge students to write poems that use a gerund in the subject position to create poems with a repeating pattern. For example: *Piano playing is . . .*

Topic Variations

You can change the assignment to be about a different memory. Students can write "I Remember" poems for:

• a specific person.

• a specific place visited on vacation.

• a favorite television character.

Writing About Literature

Students can compose "I Remember" poems about the memories of a literary character, such as

• Charlotte's memories of her trip across the Atlantic in *The True Confessions of Charlotte Doyle*.

• Bo's memories of the anger-management class in *Ironman*.

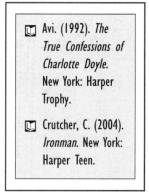

📖 Avi. (1992). *The True Confessions of Charlotte Doyle.* New York: Harper Trophy.

📖 Crutcher, C. (2004). *Ironman.* New York: Harper Teen.

Three Wishes
by Karla Kuskin

Three wishes	1
Three.	2
The first	3
A tree:	4
Dark bark	5
Green leaves	6
Under a bit of blue	7
A canopy	8
To glimpse sky through	9
To watch sun sift through	10
To catch light rain	11
Upon the leaves	12
And let it fall again.	13
A place to put my eye	14
Beyond the window frame.	15
Wish two:	16
A chair	17
Not hard or high	18
One that fits comfortably	19
Set by the window tree	20
An island in the room	21
For me	22
My own	23
Place to sit and be	24
Alone.	25
My tree	26
There.	27
Here my chair,	28
Me,	29
Rain, sky, sun.	30
All my wishes	31
All the things I need	32
But one	33
Wish three:	34
A book to read.	35

© 1975, 1980 by Karla Kuskin.

Teaching Grammar With Perfect Poems for Middle School • Scholastic Teaching Resources

Three Wishes Poems

¤ ¤ ¤ ¤ ¤ ¤ **Instructional Objective** ¤ ¤ ¤ ¤ ¤ ¤ ¤

Students write a "Three Wishes" poem that contains nine infinitives.

Source Poem: "Three Wishes" by Karla Kuskin (reproducible page 44)

Introductory Activity

Distribute copies of "Three Wishes" by Karla Kuskin. Read the poem once to the class. Assign students to underline or highlight the three phrases beginning with *to* in the first stanza of the poem. Have students read these *to* phrases in unison as you read the rest of the lines.

Modeling Activity

Imitate the model poem so that it reflects a different point of view, such as that of a football coach, cook, bus driver, or someone else whom students all know. Let the class choose the point of view and have students brainstorm a list of things that the person might wish for, such as new uniforms, a winning season, or a perfect place kicker. Have the class choose the three best wishes. Select one or more of the ideas from the brainstorming list and model how to begin a phrase with the word *to*. For example, *new uniforms: to inspire pride, to intimidate the other teams, to look their best in their sports-page picture.* Have students each select one of the three wishes and compose one line.

Create a class poem by recording lines on the board or overhead. Adapt Kuskin's opening to begin the class poem: "Three wishes. The first a _____." Accept volunteered lines, and help students revise the lines to

> **TIP**
>
> Since the point of the modeling activity is to imitate the grammar element rather than the sound element, it is not necessary that the lines of the class poem rhyme. Students can attempt rhyme later for a revision activity.

follow the pattern of *to* plus an action. When you have three lines for each of the three wishes, conclude with the line "Three wishes." You might publish the class poem in the school newsletter.

Grammar Mini-Lesson

Four ways to define infinitives are listed below. Consider which explanations will help your particular students.

TIP

Use an analogy to explain infinitives: Just as a vampire needs two fangs to be considered a vampire, an infinitive needs to have the word *to* in order to be considered an infinitive. Without two fangs, vampires look like magicians, and without the word *to*, infinitives are just verbs (Carrie Melon).

Function:
An infinitive is a verb with the word *to* preceding it. An infinitive phrase contains the infinitive plus any extra words, such as direct objects or adjectives.

I want a tree *to catch* light rain.	*infinitive*
I want a tree *to catch light rain*.	*infinitive phrase*

Although it contains a verb, an infinitive is not a true verb. Instead, it's called a verbal and functions as another part of speech, such as a noun, adjective, or an adverb. Infinitive phrases can be found in several places in a sentence.

The tree needs *to catch* light rain.	noun, the direct object of *needs*.
I want a tree *to catch* light rain.	adjective, modifying the noun *tree*.
The tree is leafy *to catch* light rain.	adverb, modifying the adjective *leafy*.

Meaning:
Infinitives provide a way to speak about actions as topics. Because they are made from verbs, infinitives are livelier than regular nouns, adjectives, and adverbs. Skilled writers can use infinitive phrases for sentence variety and to further describe and qualify the action being discussed.

Identification:
An infinitive always begins with *to*. Check to see if the word following *to* is a verb. If the element begins with *to* and is followed by a verb, it is an infinitive.

I want a tree *to catch* light rain.   *Catch* is a verb following *to*.

Example:
Have students identify the six infinitive phrases in Kuskin's poem: *to glimpse sky through, to watch sun sift through, to catch light rain, to put my eye, to sit and be,* and *to read.*

Prewriting for an Individual Pattern Poem

Students can write "Three Wishes" poems for their own wishes. Have students each brainstorm a list of objects or experiences that would cause a positive change in their lives. Encourage students to select objects or experiences that are free or intangible, such as a day on the beach or a word of praise from a respected person. Have students select their three favorite objects or experiences and brainstorm three actions that could be associated with each one.

Writing the Poem

Have students draft their own poems, imitating the repeating *to*-phrase pattern of the original model. Use the frame below as a guide.

Poem Frame

Three wishes   1

The first a/an _____: 2
          (object)

To _____   3
      (action phrase)

To _____   4
      (action phrase)

To _____   5
      (action phrase)

The second a/an _____: 6
          (object)

To _____   7
      (action phrase)

To _____   8
      (action phrase)

To _____   9
      (action phrase)

The third a/an _____: 10
          (object)

To _____   11
      (action phrase)

To _____   12
      (action phrase)

To _____   13
      (action phrase)

Three wishes   14

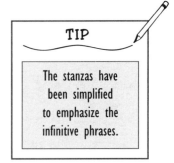

TIP

The stanzas have been simplified to emphasize the infinitive phrases.

Publishing Activity: Wish Bottle

TIP

Make aged-looking paper by sponging strong coffee or tea onto the page.

- Glue or tape colored card stock or foil to an empty cylindrical potato chip container.
- From the same paper as the covering, cut out a bottle shape (wide bottom, narrow top) to create a façade that will change the appearance of the can. Decorate the bottle shape with ribbon or markers and attach it to the can with a rubber band or elastic.
- Cover the lid with foil and attach a plastic ornament on top with wire.
- Print out the poem and roll the page into a tube. Place the poem in the wish bottle.

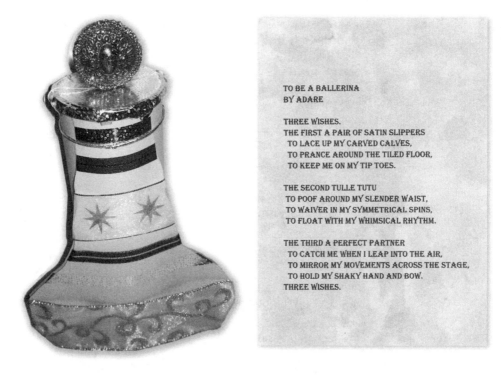

TO BE A BALLERINA
BY ADARE

THREE WISHES.
THE FIRST A PAIR OF SATIN SLIPPERS
    TO LACE UP MY CARVED CALVES,
    TO PRANCE AROUND THE TILED FLOOR,
    TO KEEP ME ON MY TIP TOES.

THE SECOND TULLE TUTU
    TO POOF AROUND MY SLENDER WAIST,
    TO WAIVER IN MY SYMMETRICAL SPINS,
    TO FLOAT WITH MY WHIMSICAL RHYTHM.

THE THIRD A PERFECT PARTNER
    TO CATCH ME WHEN I LEAP INTO THE AIR,
    TO MIRROR MY MOVEMENTS ACROSS THE STAGE,
    TO HOLD MY SHAKY HAND AND BOW.
THREE WISHES.

Critical-Thinking Time

The thought teasers are provided for your students to discuss in small groups and then share with the whole class for further wondering and discussion.

- The infinitives in Kuskin's first stanza follow the typical pattern: *to*, a verb, and a direct object. Write down the infinitive phrase from the second stanza and tell what is different about it. Repeat for the infinitive in the last stanza. (To sit and be alone *is a compound verb infinitive. To read* is an infinitive without a direct object.)

❖ The stanzas in this poem are not sentences. Write a complete sentence with the infinitive *to read*. (*A possible answer: I love to read.*)

❖ Most infinitives use action verbs but it is possible to use state-of-being verbs as infinitives. Write a sentence with the infinitive *to be*. (*A possible answer: She likes to be alone.*)

❖ Say the famous Shakespearean quote with the *to be* infinitive. (*To be or not to be: that is the question.*)

Grammar Reinforcement Activity

Use the following activity to reinforce the structure and function of infinitives and provide an opportunity to discuss additional information or confusing features.

Divide the class into two groups to play Name That Tune. To prepare, have students in each group write popular song titles that have "to" phrases in their titles, such as "To Dream the Impossible Dream," "Born to Be Wild," and "Getting to Know You." On each round, have one group present a song to the other group, which must guess the title. Score one point for each correct guess. For a bonus round, require titles that contain infinitive phrases and are a specific number of words in length. The group with the most points wins.

Grammar Extension Activity

An additional concept about infinitives can be introduced to students who want to learn more, or this activity can be used for an extra-credit assignment.

Three Types of "To" Phrases:
Infinitive phrases begin with the preposition *to*. Two other sentence elements that can also begin with *to* are prepositional phrases and indirect objects.

Infinitive phrase   She gave the tickets *to go* to France to him.
Prepositional phrase   She gave the tickets to go *to France* to him.
Indirect object phrase She gave the tickets to go to France *to him*.

Challenge students to write a sentence like the one above that has three different types of "to" phrases: infinitive, prepositional, and indirect object.

Topic Variations

You can focus the assignment on writing from different points of view. Students can write "Three Wishes" poems for:

- a relative or specific person.
- a personified object that is mistreated by humans.
- an endangered animal or global location.

Writing About Literature

Students can compose "Three Wishes" poems about a literary character such as

- Emily in *Toning the Sweep*.
- Maniac in *Maniac Magee*.

📖 Johnson, A. (1994). *Toning the Sweep*. New York: Scholastic.

📖 Spinelli, J. (2002). *Maniac Magee*. New York: Scholastic.

Dumb and Dumber
by Bruce Lansky

It's dumber than taking a shower,   1

before you've removed all your clothes.   2

It's dumber than petting a lion.   3

It's dumber than picking your nose.   4

It's dumber than wiping your nose on your sleeve,   5

then wiping your sleeve on your pants.   6

It's dumber than dressing in diapers   7

when you take a date to a dance.   8

It's dumber than sharing an apple,   9

with several hungry worms.   10

It's dumber than sharing a cookie   11

with a friend who is loaded with germs.   12

It's dumber than saying that you can't stand   13

a person whom you've never met.   14

What's dumber by far than all of these things   15

is smoking your first cigarette.   16

© 2000 by Bruce Lansky.

Teaching Grammar With Perfect Poems for Middle School • Scholastic Teaching Resources

Comparison Poems

> ⌧ ⌧ ⌧ ⌧ ⌧ ⌧ **Instructional Objective** ⌧ ⌧ ⌧ ⌧ ⌧ ⌧
>
> Students write a "Comparison" poem that contains one repeating comparative adjective.
>
> Source Poem: "Dumb and Dumber" by Bruce Lansky (reproducible page 51)

Introductory Activity

Distribute copies of "Dumb and Dumber" by Bruce Lansky. Read the poem aloud to the class. For a second reading, assign individual students to read aloud one of the eight "It's" statements and one student to read the last two lines. Afterward, have the class read the poem again, this time with students on the left side of the room reading only "It's dumber" (the beginning of each statement), and students on the right side of the room reading the rest of each statement. Have the whole class read the last two lines.

Modeling Activity

Imitate the model poem for other foolish or forgetful actions such as breaking school rules or mixing up morning routines. Assign students to write one statement beginning with "It's dumber than." Start by having students brainstorm a list of unwise actions that would result in negative consequences, such as being tardy, talking out of turn, or mistaking the wrong tube for toothpaste. Select one of the ideas from the brainstorming

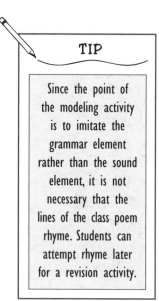

TIP

Since the point of the modeling activity is to imitate the grammar element rather than the sound element, it is not necessary that the lines of the class poem rhyme. Students can attempt rhyme later for a revision activity.

list and model how to create a two-line statement with specific details: *It's dumber than sauntering into the office at 11 o'clock because you overslept for the third time this week* or *It's dumber than squirting acne medicine on your toothbrush because you played video games until 2 a.m.* Tell students that adding *when*, *then*, *because*, *while*, *that*, or *who* at the beginning of the second line will help with adding more detail. Have each student select a favorite item from the class list and compose a two-line statement on a small strip of paper.

Select eight volunteers to write their statements with overhead markers onto 2-inch strips cut from clear acetate or transparency sheets. Place the strips on the overhead to create a class poem. Take suggestions from the class for the order of the lines. Lines can be grouped by similar topics or in chronological order or from least to most important. Use the author's last two lines to end the poem: "What's dumber by far than *each* of these things is smoking your first cigarette." Technically, the dumber comparison should be between *two* things instead of *all of these things*. You may want to create a new ending statement using the superlative form of the adjective: "What's dumb*est* by far of all these things is smoking your first cigarette." The class poem could be published by sending it to the local cancer association.

Grammar Mini-Lesson

Four ways to define comparative adjectives are listed below. Consider which explanations will help your particular students.

Function:
A comparative adjective compares a quality between two things. In a sentence the comparative adjective is usually located somewhere between the two items being compared. A superlative adjective compares a quality among three or more things.

It's *dumber* than petting a lion.	compares *it* and *petting a lion*
Smoking is the *dumbest* thing of all.	compares *smoking* and all the things in the poem

Meaning:
Comparative adjectives set up a comparison and are used for description to indicate superiority or inferiority in quality, quantity, or intensity. Beginning writers can include comparative adjectives with *than* to add similes to their writing.

TIP

Use an analogy to explain comparative adjectives. Comparative and superlative adjectives are like people who brag. Comparative adjectives think they are bettER, and superlatives think that they are the bEST. The word *comparative* has the sound of *pair* in it which means "two" and *superlative* has the word *super* which means "best."

Identification:
A comparative adjective often ends with -*er*. Since it is hard to pronounce a long word with -*er* on the end, an adjective with two or more syllables usually uses the word *more* in front of it: *more alert*, not *alerter*. If the element has -*er* behind it or *more* in front, it is a comparative adjective.

Example:
Have students identify the comparative adjective in Lansky's poem. The comparative adjective that is repeated several times in the poem is *dumber*.

Prewriting for an Individual Pattern Poem

Students can write their own "Comparison" poems for actions of their choice. As a class, brainstorm a list of places, such as home, school, restaurant, mall, theater, zoo, amusement park, ballpark, beauty salon, court, car, jungle, and desert. Have students select eight or more places to create a corresponding list of dumb actions to match the chosen places. Have the class brainstorm a list of serious health risks or other warnings for the last two lines.

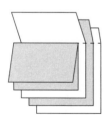

Writing the Poem

Have students draft their own poems, imitating the repeating "It's dumber than" pattern of the original model. Use the frame on page 55 as a guide.

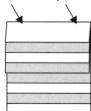

Fold and staple here.

Publishing Activity: Step Book

- Set four sheets of $8\frac{1}{2}$- by 11-inch paper (two of one color and two of another) in a stack, oriented vertically, with each page positioned 1 inch below the next.

- Holding all the sheets together, fold the pages over so that there are eight descending 1-inch strips. Staple the top fold to hold all the pages in place.

- Each strip can hold two lines of text handwritten or glued in place. Extra paper can be stapled to the top from behind to hold the "face" title and author's name (see photo on page 55).

Poem Frame

It's dumber than _____   1
                       (action)

when you _____.   2
          (action at a place)

It's dumber than _____.   3
                       (action)

It's dumber than _____.   4
                       (action)

It's dumber than _____   5
                       (action)

then _____.   6
          (another action)

It's dumber than _____   7
                       (action)

when you _____.   8
          (action at a place)

It's dumber than _____   9
                       (action)

when you _____.   10
          (action at a place)

It's dumber than _____   11
                       (action)

when you _____.   12
          (action at a place)

It's dumber than _____   13
                       (action)

when _____.   14
          (action at a place)

What's dumbest by far of all these things   15

is_____.   16
          (action)

Dumb and Dumber
by Niki

It's dumber than not doing your homework
when you know that it's half of your grade.

It's dumber than playing with mountains of matches.
It's dumber than kissing a sickening toad.

It's dumber than gorging on gobs of garlic
then going on a romantic date.

It's dumber than munching ten McDonald's Big Macs
when you're already one hundred pounds overweight.

It's dumber than drinking ten cups of caffeinated coffee
when your bedtime is in less than an hour.

It's dumber than chomping six sumptuous chocolate bars
when your mom is cooking a four-course meal.

It's dumber than falling asleep for five hours
when you're lying out in the smoldering sun.

What's dumbest by far than all of these things
is the belief that you can't do something.

TIP

The last two lines have been changed to include the superlative form of the adjective.

Critical-Thinking Time

The thought teasers are provided for your students to discuss in small groups and then share with the whole class for further wondering and discussion.

- Find a word that appears with *dumber* in each statement in Lansky's poem. (*The word* than *is usually paired with comparative adjectives.*) Next, find the statement that has both *than* and *then*, and explain the function of both words. (*Lines five and six contain both words.* Than *makes a comparison, and* then *signals the next action in a sequence.*)

- Lansky's statements usually begin with *it's*. Determine what word or phrase the pronoun *it* is referring to (the antecedent). Explain what effect this repetition has for the reader. (*The referent for* it *is smoking your first cigarette. By not revealing what is referred to until the end of the poem, Lansky causes the reader to wonder what is worse than the listed actions.*)

- *Dumber* is a comparative adjective. Create an original definition that describes a comparative adjective by saying that it is like something else. (*Possible answers: A comparative adjective is like an advertisement because it compares two things, or a comparative adjective is like a contest judge because it makes comparisons.*)

Grammar Reinforcement Activity

Use the following activity to reinforce the basic concept and provide an opportunity to discuss additional information or confusing features.

Group students into teams of three to play Guess Our Pictures with comparative adjectives. Give each group three tablets or dry-erase boards and markers. Have each group randomly select a card from a stack of comparative adjective cards. After a brief discussion the group members should each draw a picture to represent one of the three forms of the adjective: base, comparative, and superlative. Groups can each draw different objects or they can draw the same object and just draw more details on the object. After three minutes, the groups should stand in a line and hold up their drawings to the class. Then, the rest of the students can guess the adjective. Repeat several times; the group with the most correct answers wins.

Grammar Extension Activity

An additional concept about comparative adjectives can be introduced to students who want to learn more, or this activity can be used for an extra-credit assignment.

More or Most:
Words of two or more syllables may take *more* or *most* rather than -er or -est, as with *more unusual* and *most unusual*. When in doubt, always look up the word in the dictionary because the dictionary will tell if the word takes a suffix or a form of *more*.

Irregular Adjectives:
Adjectives like *good* and *bad* are the hardest for students to learn since the comparative and superlative forms may break from the prevailing pattern and change to different words. The chart displays these words:

Irregular Adjectives		
Base Adjectives	**Comparative Adjective**	**Superlative Adjective**
good	better	best
bad	worse	worst
much	more	most
little	less	least
only	only	only

Students might be encouraged to know that overgeneralizations like *gooder* and *bestest* are hypercorrections based on the brain's logical theory about adjectives. The brain logically assumes that these forms would follow the same pattern. It just takes a little more attention to get the brain to learn a different pattern. Challenge students to write poems that use an adjective that takes *most*, such as *The most unusual thing in the world is . . .* or that uses another irregular adjective alone, such as *The worst thing in the world is . . .*

Topic Variations

You can change the central comparative adjective in the poem. Students can write "Comparison" poems with:

- *smarter*, to praise a favorite person: *My brother is smarter than 12 computers.*

- *stronger*, to build a resume for a superhero: *The Incredible Hulk is stronger than an Abrams tank.*

- *softer*, to advertise a product: *Makes your skin softer than rose petals.*

Writing About Literature

Students can compose "Comparison" poems that describe the traits of literary characters, such as

- Karana's bravery in *Island of the Blue Dolphins*.

- Brian's will to survive in *Hatchet*.

O'Dell, S. (1971). *Island of the Blue Dolphins*. New York: Dell Yearling.

Paulsen, G. (1996). *Hatchet*. New York: Aladdin.

Harriet Tubman
by Sharon Lindsey

Harriet Tubman, you were heroic.   1

You were glorious and resistant.   2

You were dedicated and fearless.   3

You were loyal and persistent.   4

How we exclaimed with admiration   5

When you fought for abolition.   6

Then you freed three hundred slaves,   7

Saying, "I will never end my mission!"   8

You were sneaky, Harriet Tubman.   9

You were clandestine and sly.   10

You were brave and defiant.   11

You were wonderful and kind.   12

Even when you were unhealthy,   13

You were sure to keep your cool.   14

We were never disappointed.   15

Harriet Tubman, we adore you.   16

© 2006 by Sharon Lindsey.

Teaching Grammar With Perfect Poems for Middle School • Scholastic Teaching Resources

Greatest Person Poems

¤ ¤ ¤ ¤ ¤ ¤ **Instructional Objective** ¤ ¤ ¤ ¤ ¤ ¤

Students write a "Greatest Person" poem that contains 15 predicate adjectives.

Source Poem: "Harriet Tubman" by Sharon Lindsey (reproducible page 59)

Introductory Activity

Distribute copies of "Harriet Tubman" by Sharon Lindsey. Read the poem aloud to the class. Assign students to underline or highlight all the words in the poem that describe Harriet Tubman. Ask for two volunteers to share all the descriptive words they've marked and have the class confirm their choices or discuss any words missed or incorrectly marked. Once the class is in agreement about the descriptive words, assign one of the volunteers to read the first stanza and the other to read the second stanza, pausing for the whole class to read the descriptive words. (See the Grammar Mini-Lesson for answers.) Conduct a class reading of the poem, with individuals reading the descriptive words and the class reading the rest of the lines.

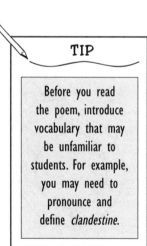

TIP

Before you read the poem, introduce vocabulary that may be unfamiliar to students. For example, you may need to pronounce and define *clandestine*.

Modeling Activity

Imitate the model poem for a new greatest person. Assign students to write a sentence with this pattern: "You were _____ and _____." Have the class select a subject they all know, such as a media personality, community member, or favorite author. Create two columns on the board: Accomplishments and Description. Have students brainstorm several descriptive words for each accomplishment. You may want to do a mini-lesson on using the thesaurus. Tell students to select one accomplishment for their line.

Create a class poem together on the board or overhead. Write the first and last lines using the person's name. Decide on two or three accomplishments to include in the poem. Accept volunteers' suggestions for the descriptive words until the stanzas are complete. Revise any lines that do not contain two descriptive words. You might publish the class poem by mailing it to the admired person.

Grammar Mini-Lesson

Four ways to define predicate adjectives are listed below. Consider which explanations will help your particular students.

Function:
A predicate adjective is a descriptive word that follows a linking verb and that describes something about the subject. If the adjective is placed in front of the noun it is just an adjective.

You were *heroic*.   *predicate adjective*
Heroic Harriet Tubman fought for freedom.   *adjective*

Linking verbs imply a state or condition of being and not an action. One type of linking verb is the state-of-being verb *to be*: *is, am, are, was, were, be, being, been.* This type of linking verb is used in this poem.

You *were* heroic.   *state-of-being linking verb*

Other linking verbs are those related to the five senses: *look, sound, smell, feel, taste, appear, seem, become, grow, turn, prove, remain,* and *get.* This type of linking verb is not used in this poem.

You *sounded* happy.   *sensory linking verb*

Meaning:
Predicate adjectives emphasize the descriptive word by equating the subject with the descriptive word.

Identification:
A predicate adjective must be an adjective following a linking verb. The best way to test if it is an adjective is to put a noun after it, such

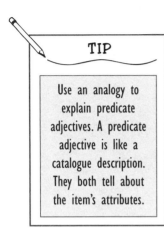

TIP

Use an analogy to explain predicate adjectives. A predicate adjective is like a catalogue description. They both tell about the item's attributes.

as a *person*, *place*, or *thing*, to see if it makes sense. If the element is an adjective and follows a linking verb, it is a predicate adjective.

You were (a) *heroic* (person).   "Heroic" is an adjective following a linking verb.

Example:
Have students identify the predicate adjectives in Lindsey's poem: *heroic, glorious, resistant, dedicated, fearless, loyal, persistent, sneaky, clandestine, sly, brave, defiant, wonderful, kind, unhealthy, sure,* and *disappointed*.

Prewriting for an Individual Pattern Poem

Students can write their own "Greatest Person" poems for special people. Have students individually create lists of notable people in their lives, community, nation, and world. Share their lists as a class. Have students select a favorite person and create a two-column list of accomplishments and corresponding descriptions. Students should strive for 16 or more descriptive words for their person. Students can also list exclamations this person may have uttered.

Writing the Poem

Have students draft their own poems, imitating the repeating "You were" pattern of the original model. Use the frame on page 63 as a guide.

Publishing Activity: Medal of Honor Tin

TIP

Metal cases often come free with a promotional CD for dial-up Internet service.

• You'll need a 5- by 5½-inch metal CD case and a small yogurt lid 3 inches in diameter. Trace the CD cover shape onto colored card stock twice. Cut out one shape and label it "Medal of Honor" in fancy print or with letter stickers. Attach this cover to the front of the CD with double-sided tape. Cut the second shape smaller to fit inside the lid, and secure it in place with tape (this is the inside cover).

• Cover the yogurt lid with foil and a sticker and attach a ribbon to the back to represent a medal of honor. Glue the medal to the inner cover.

• On white or colored printer paper, write or print out the poem to fit to the size of the case. Place the case over the poem and trace around it. Trim the paper to fit inside the bottom of the CD case. Secure the poem to the inside back cover with double-sided tape.

Poem Frame

_____ _____, you were _____.   1
  (first)   (last name)   (description)

You were _____ and _____.   2
              (description)   (description)

You were _____ and _____.   3
              (description)   (description)

You were _____ and _____.   4
              (description)   (description)

How I exclaimed with _____   5
                              (emotion)

When you _____.   6
              (accomplishment)

Then you _____,   7
              (accomplishment)

Saying, "I _____!"   8
                (exclamation)

You were _____, _____ _____.   9
              (description)   (first)   (last name)

You were _____ and _____.   10
              (description)   (description)

You were _____ and _____.   11
              (description)   (description)

You were _____ and _____.   12
              (description)   (description)

Even when you were _____,   13
                          (description)

You were sure to _____.   14
                        (reaction)

I was never disappointed.   15

_____ _____, I adore you.   16
  (first)   (last name)

Critical-Thinking Time

The thought teasers are provided for your students to discuss in small groups and then share with the whole class for further wondering and discussion.

- Lindsey set up the pattern of lines with two predicate adjectives joined by *and*. List the four lines that have only one predicate adjective. (*Harriet Tubman, you were heroic; Even when you were unhealthy, You were sure to keep your cool;* and *We were never disappointed.*)

- There are three predicate adjectives in this poem that may not appear to be adjectives: *dedicated, sure,* and *disappointed.* Select one and list three reasons why this word is an adjective. (*Possible answers:* Dedicated *describes her.* Dedicated *can be placed in front of Harriet. And* heroic *could be substituted for* dedicated.)

- Lindsey's poem has another interesting sentence element. Her poem has three nouns of direct address. Without being given a definition, find the three nouns of direct address and make up a definition that would explain the term. (*Lines 1, 9, and 16 have nouns of direct address. A noun of direct address is a person's name that is used to address the person directly. This is added onto a complete sentence and is not the subject or object of the sentence.*)

Grammar Reinforcement Activity

Use the following activity to reinforce students' understanding of predicate adjectives and provide an opportunity to discuss additional information or confusing features.

To prepare for a game of Advertising Agency, make game cards by pasting on filing cards pictures of products cut from magazines and catalogues. Divide the class into small groups, or agencies. Have each agency draw one product card and compose in two minutes as many predicate adjective sentences for the product as they can. The team that creates the most predicate adjective sentences scores one point. Repeat for several rounds; the team with the most points wins. For fun, include some items that would be difficult to sell.

Grammar Extension Activity

An additional concept about predicate adjectives can be introduced to students who want to learn more, or this activity can be used for an extra-credit assignment.

Sensory Linking Verbs:

Predicate adjectives follow linking verbs. In Lindsey's poem the only linking verb used is the state-of-being linking verb *were*. The linking verbs related to the five senses are: *look, sound, smell, feel, taste, appear, seem, become, grow, turn, prove, remain,* and *get*.

You *were* brave and defiant.   *state-of-being linking verb*
You *became* impatient and unhappy.   *sensory linking verb*

Challenge students to write a poem for a favorite object using sensory linking verbs.

Topic Variations

You can change the assignment to be about a different type of person. Students can write "Greatest Person" poems for:

• a famous inventor or historical person.

• a famous artist or musician.

• a contemporary person in a recent news story.

Writing About Literature

Students can compose "Greatest Person" poems for a literary character, such as

• Moose in *Al Capone Does My Shirts*.

• Billie Jo in *Out of the Dust*.

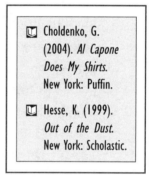

Choldenko, G. (2004). *Al Capone Does My Shirts.* New York: Puffin.

Hesse, K. (1999). *Out of the Dust.* New York: Scholastic.

I Will Never Completely Grow Up
by Sara Britton

I am a Rainbow Brite girl,   1

jumping to the tunes of Michael Jackson,   2

Jazzercising with Barbie,   3

and strutting my stuff with striped leg warmers and a slap-on bracelet.   4

I am a Lite-Brite painter,   5

building fine architectural restaurants from Legos,   6

creating a make-believe world of Little People,   7

and pretending to play store in my bedroom with a good friend   8
  and a smile.

I am not a magazine girl,   9

bursting from my size-two jeans,   10

coloring my hair every four weeks,   11

and getting lost in the idea that looks are everything and after 30,   12
  it's all downhill.

I am a Care Bear girl, Princess of Power girl, and not a size two,   13
  Abercrombie model.

Legos have never died, and a make-believe world lies outside the box of   14
  the TV and Playstation.

The times might catch up with me, but I will never completely grow up.   15

© 2005 by Sara Britton.

Teaching Grammar With Perfect Poems for Middle School • Scholastic Teaching Resources

I Am Poems

¤ ¤ ¤ ¤ ¤ ¤ **Instructional Objective** ¤ ¤ ¤ ¤ ¤ ¤

Students write an "I Am" poem that contains nine participial phrases.

Source Poem: "I Will Never Completely Grow Up" by Sara Britton (reproducible page 66)

Introductory Activity

Distribute copies of "I Will Never Completely Grow Up" by Sara Britton. Read aloud the poem. Have students underline or highlight all the lines containing an action word that ends in *-ing*. Ask volunteers to each select one of these lines to read. Conduct a class reading in which you read the first line of each stanza and the last three lines of the poem and the volunteers read their *-ing* lines. Read the poem again, permitting each volunteer to select another student to read the line with him or her.

Modeling Activity

Imitate the model poem for some experience that students have in common, such as being from the same state, town, or generation. When the class has selected a topic, work together to create a list on the board of five or more lines beginning with *I am* and showing students' relationship to the topic. For example, *I am an Ohio State fan* might be an appropriate opening line for a state poem. Have students select one "I am" statement from the list and individually brainstorm several *-ing* actions. Model one or two lines before asking students to create their own. A student who chose to describe him- or herself as an Ohio State fan, for example, might add *wearing scarlet and gray to watch every game and cheering my team on to victory*. You may want to challenge students to write lines with several details. Group students together with the same "I am" statements to create a stanza.

Have each group share their stanza by reading the "I am" line followed by their individual *-ing* lines. For the last line of the poem, create a cumulative list of the topics of all the stanzas. The class poem could be shared with parents. Parents could respond in kind by writing about their generation.

Grammar Mini-Lesson

Four ways to define participial phrases are listed below. Consider which explanations will help your particular students.

Function:
A participle is a verb form with an *-ing* or *-ed* ending. A participial phrase is a participle plus any other words associated with it, such as direct objects or prepositional phrases. A participial phrase adds extra information to a complete sentence and functions as an adjective that usually describes or modifies the subject or object of the sentence. Participial phrases can be found in several places in a sentence.

I am not a magazine girl, *bursting from my size two jeans.*
  participial phrase modifies *girl*

Bursting from my size two jeans, I decided not to eat another bite.
  participial phrase modifies *I*

Meaning:
Participial phrases provide a way for lengthy descriptive information to be attached to the main clause of a sentence. Advanced writers use participial phrases for sentence variety and to compose long sentences with lots of interesting details.

Identification:
A participle usually is a verb with an *-ing* ending; however, the verb can have an *-ed* ending or be an irregular verb form. Since words with an *-ing* ending can also be verbs or gerunds, the best way to test for them is to drop the phrase and see if the sentence makes sense without it. Participial phrases are additional to the sentence and can be dropped. Participial phrases always take a comma or commas to set them off as additional to the main sentence. If the element begins with a participle, can be dropped, and is set off with comma(s), it is a participial phrase.

I am not a magazine girl, ~~bursting from my size two jeans.~~
The participial phrase can be dropped and the sentence still makes sense.

Example:
Have students identify the participial phrases in Britton's poem: *jumping to the tunes of Michael Jackson, Jazzercising with Barbie, strutting my stuff with striped leg warmers and a slap-on bracelet, building fine architectural*

TIP

Use an analogy to explain participial phrases. Participial phrases are like ice cream sprinkles that are added onto a complete dessert. Like the sprinkles, participial phrases can be left off but the complete sentence is much better with the extra details.

restaurants from Legos, creating a make-believe world of Little People, pretending to play store in my bedroom with a good friend and a smile, bursting from my size two jeans, coloring my hair every four weeks, getting lost in the idea that looks are everything and after 30, and it's all downhill.

Prewriting for an Individual Pattern Poem

Students can write their own "I Am" poems about themselves. Have students individually create lists of favorite childhood toys, games, and pastimes. Have them make a second list of least favorite adult media stereotypes. Students can further develop their childhood favorites by listing *-ing* action phrases.

Writing the Poem

Have students draft their own poems, imitating the repeating "I am" pattern of the original model. Use the frame on page 70 as a guide.

Publishing Activity: Pop-Up Card

- Download and print free pictures of both a toy storefront and several toys from the Internet. You may also draw these or cut them out from newspaper advertisements and fliers.

- Enlarge the storefront image to 7 by 5 inches on the copier or in a word-processing program. Trim and label it "Toy Store" with fancy print or stickers.

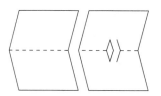

- Fold two new sheets of card stock in half horizontally. Glue the store image to the front of one card.

- On the fold of the second card, cut two 1-inch slits about 1 inch apart. Fold the tab back and forth to create a step pop-up. Push the step section to the inside of the card. Glue one toy picture to the riser, or front of the step, so that the card will fold shut.

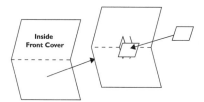

- Glue other toy pictures and a copy of the poem to the inside of the card.

- Put glue on the inside of the first card, which serves as a cover for the second card. Glue the cards together to create a single card with the toy store image on the cover and the pop-up toy image and the poem inside.

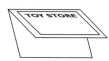

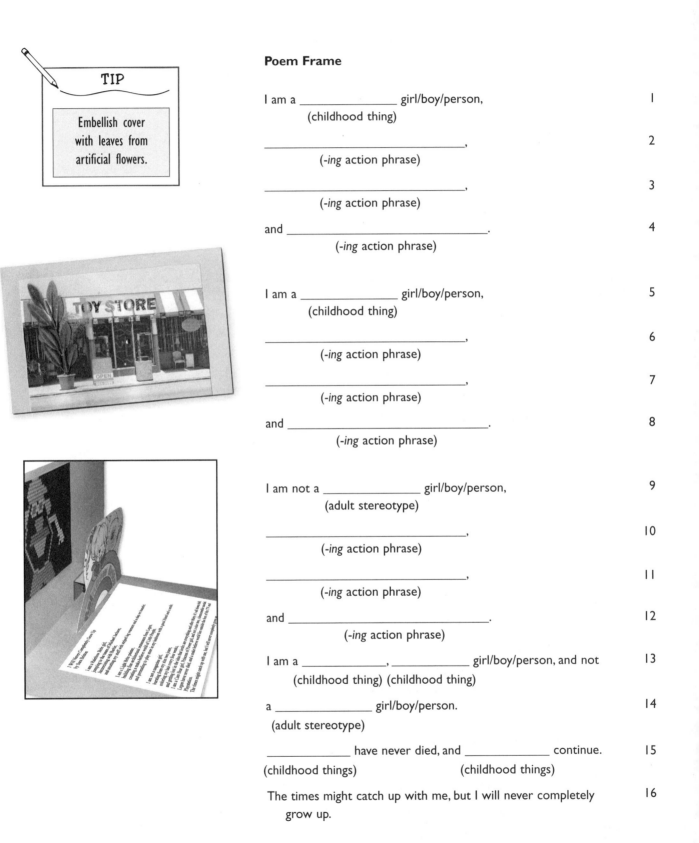

TIP

Embellish cover with leaves from artificial flowers.

Poem Frame

I am a _____ girl/boy/person,   1
    (childhood thing)

_____,   2
       (-*ing* action phrase)

_____,   3
       (-*ing* action phrase)

and _____.   4
       (-*ing* action phrase)

I am a _____ girl/boy/person,   5
    (childhood thing)

_____,   6
       (-*ing* action phrase)

_____,   7
       (-*ing* action phrase)

and _____.   8
       (-*ing* action phrase)

I am not a _____ girl/boy/person,   9
    (adult stereotype)

_____,   10
       (-*ing* action phrase)

_____,   11
       (-*ing* action phrase)

and _____.   12
       (-*ing* action phrase)

I am a _____, _____ girl/boy/person, and not   13
    (childhood thing) (childhood thing)

a _____ girl/boy/person.   14
  (adult stereotype)

_____ have never died, and _____ continue.   15
(childhood things)   (childhood things)

The times might catch up with me, but I will never completely   16
    grow up.

Critical-Thinking Time

The thought teasers are provided for your students to discuss in small groups and then share with the whole class for further wondering and discussion.

- Britton placed all of the participial phrases at the end of her sentences. However, where the participial phrase is placed can change the meaning of the sentence. Tell how the meaning is changed when the participial phrase is moved in these sentences:

    Wearing leg warmers, I Jazzercised with Barbie.

    I Jazzercised with Barbie, wearing leg warmers.

    (*In the first sentence* I *am wearing the leg warmers and in the second one* Barbie *is wearing them.*)

- Each of the following sentences ends with a participial phrase:

    She enjoyed Legos, stacked to look like buildings.

    She enjoyed Legos, built into restaurants.

Explain how you can tell that each sentence has a participial phrase, and tell how these phrases are different from the ones in Britton's poem. (*Both phrases can be dropped and the sentence still makes sense. The participles have different forms:* stacked *is a verb with an* -ed *ending, and* built *is an irregular verb. Britton only used regular* -ing *verbs.*)

Grammar Reinforcement Activity

Use the following activity to reinforce the function of participial phrases and provide an opportunity to discuss additional information or confusing features.

Divide students into groups of four to write a chain superhero poem. Have each group use one sheet of paper divided into fourths accordion-style, from top to bottom. Have the first person choose a superhero and write a sentence at the *top of a sheet of paper, following the pattern:* _____ *is a superhero.* Have each of the three remaining group members add a participial phrase under the kernel sentence. Share the poems by reading them aloud. For fun, repeat the process with each person folding over the part they've written so that the next person cannot read the previous part.

Grammar Extension Activity

An additional concept about participial phrases can be introduced to students who are ready to learn more, or this activity can be used for an extra-credit assignment.

Punctuating Participial Phrases:
When used in sentences, participial phrases always take commas. Sara Britton's poem places the participial phrases after the kernel sentence. Participial phrases can also be placed before a kernel sentence or even in the middle of a sentence.

She found her childhood toys, *sitting on the top closet shelf.*
Sitting on the top closet shelf, the toys were totally out of sight.
The toys, *sitting on the top closet shelf,* had been forgotten for years.

Challenge students to write three sentences, each with a participial phrase in a different location: before, after, and in the middle of a kernel sentence. Remind students to punctuate the participial phrases with commas.

Topic Variations

Invite students to write the poem from a different point of view. Students can write "I Am" poems for:

• a common, everyday object.

• a famous painting.

• an object from an older family member's childhood.

📖 Peck, R. (2000). *A Long Way From Chicago.* New York: Puffin.

📖 Peck, R. (2002). *A Year Down Yonder.* New York: Puffin.

Writing About Literature

Students can compose "I Am" poems about a literary character's experiences, such as

• Joey's experiences as a grandchild in *A Long Way From Chicago.*

• Mary Alice's experiences as a grandchild in *A Year Down Yonder.*

My Noisy Brother
by Bruce Lansky

My brother's such a noisy kid,	1
when he eats soup he slurps.	2
When he drinks milk he gargles.	3
And after meals he burps.	4
He cracks his knuckles when he's bored.	5
He whistles when he walks.	6
He snaps his fingers when he sings,	7
and when he's mad he squawks.	8
At night my brother snores so loud	9
it sounds just like a riot.	10
Even when he sleeps	11
my noisy brother isn't quiet.	12

© 1994 by Bruce Lansky.

Teaching Grammar With Perfect Poems for Middle School • Scholastic Teaching Resources

Time Poems

> ¤ ¤ ¤ ¤ ¤ ¤ **Instructional Objective** ¤ ¤ ¤ ¤ ¤ ¤
>
> Students write a "Time" poem that contains nine *when* clauses.
>
> Source Poem: "My Noisy Brother" by Bruce Lansky (reproducible page 73)

Introductory Activity

Distribute copies of "My Noisy Brother" by Bruce Lansky. Read the poem aloud to the class. Have students find *when* each time it appears in the poem and underline or highlight *when* plus the two- or three-word phrase that follows it. (They should underline: *when he eats soup, when he drinks milk, when he's bored, when he walks, when he sings, when he's mad, even when he sleeps.*) Read the poem aloud, having the class read the underlined sections in unison as you read the rest of the lines.

Modeling Activity

Imitate the model poem for a different trait that is annoying. Lead students in brainstorming a list of such traits—silly, lazy, ignorant, greedy, clumsy, and so on. When the class has chosen one trait, make a two-column list of common actions and matching actions that demonstrate the trait. For example, for *greedy*: *eats pizza* (column one), *takes half of the pie* (column two). Have each student select a pair of actions from the class list and compose a *when* sentence that follows this pattern:

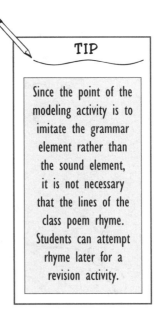

TIP

Since the point of the modeling activity is to imitate the grammar element rather than the sound element, it is not necessary that the lines of the class poem rhyme. Students can attempt rhyme later for a revision activity.

"When he_____, he_____." Point out that the action in the first column is done without the trait and begins with *when* (*When he eats pizza*), while the action in the second column is exaggerated with the bad trait (*he takes half the pie*).

Share everyone's lines by reading them aloud. Begin by reading Lansky's first line, inserting *friend* for the person and plugging in the chosen trait. Have students take turns reading their lines. Revise any lines that do not yet exaggerate the quality of the action. You can share the revised poem with another class.

Grammar Mini-Lesson

Four ways to define *when* clauses are listed below. Consider which explanations will help your particular students.

Function:
A *when* clause is a dependent or subordinate clause that depends on the main clause or the kernel sentence to function. A subordinate clause begins with a subordinate conjunction. In this poem the subordinate conjunction is *when*, and the subordinate clause serves as an adverb that modifies the whole sentence: *when* clauses are adverbial clauses. *When* clauses are usually found near the end or the beginning of a sentence.

When he eats soup, he slurps.   *subordinate clause* at the beginning of a sentence

He whistles *when he walks*.   *subordinate clause* at the end of a sentence

The addition of a subordinate clause to a main clause creates a complex sentence. Without being attached to the main clause, the subordinate clause is incomplete and is not even considered to be a sentence. A subordinate clause by itself is considered to be a fragment.

Meaning:
Subordinate clauses not only add information to a sentence, they also indicate a relationship among ideas. Beginning writers can use subordinate clauses to help them avoid fragments and run-ons. Advanced writers can use subordinate clauses to express complex ideas.

Identification:
The best way to spot a subordinate clause is to look for a subordinate conjunction such as *when*. Other subordinate conjunctions that can begin

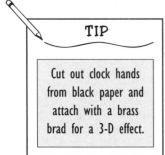

TIP

Use an analogy to explain subordinate conjunctions. Subordinate conjunctions are like glue words—they make sentences sticky and dependent; with a subordinate conjunction, a sentence turns into a dependent clause that must attach itself to a complete sentence (an independent clause). Subordinate conjunctions glue dependent clauses to independent clauses.

an adverbial clause are *whenever*, *while*, *until*, *since*, *after*, *before*, *as*, *as soon as*, and *because*. A subordinate clause can be dropped from a sentence, and the main clause will still make sense without it. If the element begins with a subordinate conjunction and can be dropped, it is a subordinate clause.

~~When he eats soup~~, he slurps.   The subordinate clause can be dropped.

Example:
Have students review the subordinate clause sentences in Lansky's poem: *when he eats soup, when he drinks milk, when he's bored, when he walks, when he sings, when he's mad,* and *when he sleeps.*

Prewriting for an Individual Pattern Poem

Students can write their own "Time" poems for qualities of their choice. As a class, brainstorm a list of both good and bad traits—overbearing, inventive, forgetful, generous, rude, neat, zany, and so on. Have each student select a favorite trait. Direct students to create an individual list of typical activities, such as combing hair, asking directions, and eating lunch. Have students make a second column in which to exaggerate the activity according to the chosen trait.

Writing the Poem

Have students draft their own poems, imitating the repeating *when* clause pattern of the original model. Use the frame on page 77 as a guide.

Publishing Activity: Clock Book

• To make the book cover, download and print or draw an analog clock face that fits the top of a frozen topping plastic lid (approximately 6 inches in diameter).

TIP

Cut out clock hands from black paper and attach with a brass brad for a 3-D effect.

• Trace around the lid on card stock to create two circles for book pages. Trim the circle pages to fit inside the lid. Tape the edges of the circles together at one point to make a binding. Fit the top circle inside the lid and secure it with double-stick tape.

• The inside of the lid/book cover becomes a credit/dedication page where a note about the poem or dedication may appear. Copy or paste a printout of the poem to the second circle, so that it appears when the book is open.

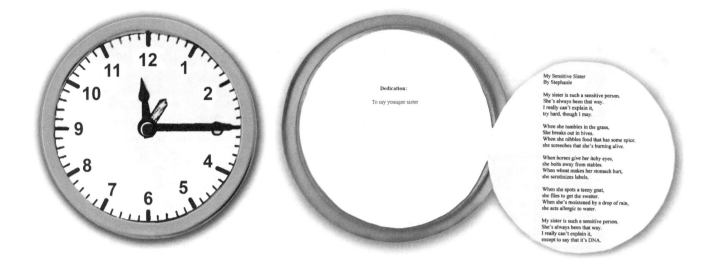

Poem Frame

My friend is such a _____ person, 1
    (quality)
when he/she _____, s/he _____. 2
    (action) (action demonstrating the quality)
When he/she _____, s/he _____. 3
    (action) (action demonstrating the quality)
And when he/she _____, s/he _____. 4
    (action) (action demonstrating the quality)

He/She _____ when s/he _____. 5
 (action demonstrating the quality) (action)
He/She _____ when s/he _____. 6
 (action demonstrating the quality) (action)
He/She _____ when s/he _____. 7
 (action demonstrating the quality) (action)
And when he/she _____ s/he _____. 8
  (action demonstrating the quality) (action)

When he/she _____, 9
    (action)
it _____like a _____. 10
 (sensory action) (comparison)
Even when he/she _____, 11
    (action)
My friend is/is not _____. 12
    (quality)

TIP

For clarity and consistency, commas have been added to the lines in which the *when* clause comes first.

Critical-Thinking Time

The thought teasers are provided for your students to discuss in small groups and then share with the whole class for further wondering and discussion.

- In the second stanza of Lansky's poem the *when* clauses are placed near the end of the sentence. Rewrite these three lines, putting the *when* clause at the beginning of the sentence. (*When he's bored, he cracks his knuckles. When he walks, he whistles. When he sings, he snaps his fingers.*)

- Lansky chose to use the same subordinate conjunction for all of the subordinate clauses. Rewrite the second stanza using some of these subordinate conjunctions to create clauses that act as adverbs: *whenever, while, until, since, after, before, as, as soon as, because.* (*Possible answers: He cracks his knuckles whenever he's bored. He whistles as he walks. He snaps his fingers while he sings. Since he's mad, he squawks.*)

- Write the instructions for taking care of a pet, using five of the subordinate conjunctions listed above. (*Possible answers: Never bother a dog while it is eating. Whenever he sits by the door, let the dog out.*)

Grammar Reinforcement Activity

Use the following activity to reinforce the function of dependent clauses and provide an opportunity to discuss additional information or confusing features.

Divide the class into teams of three to four students to play Beat the Clock. When each team has selected a cartoon character for a six-sentence story, give the team 12 index cards. Have team members write the sentences in paired clauses on the index cards so that a dependent clause beginning with *when* appears on one card and its matching independent clause appears on another (ask students to avoid using an initial capital letter or commas or periods when they write the clauses on the cards). For example: *when goofy saw the bird* (card one) / *goofy climbed the tree to get it* (card two). After each group has written six pairs of cards, have them shuffle the cards and pass them to another group. Give groups small sticky notes to use for punctuation marks and capital letters. Allow groups two minutes to match up the clauses and sentences, correctly punctuating them. Let the group that authored the cards check for correctness. If the group that authored the cards has made an error, they are disqualified. Repeat several times; the group to match and correctly edit the most sentences wins.

Grammar Extension Activity

An additional concept about *when* clauses can be introduced to students who are ready to learn more, or this activity can be used for an extra-credit assignment.

When to Use a Comma With a Subordinate Clause:
When the main clause comes before the subordinate clause, no comma is necessary. This is because the most common order for a complex sentence is to have the main clause come first. The only exception is if the information in the subordinate clause is unnecessary. However, when the subordinate clause comes first, the introductory clause should be followed by a comma. The comma signals to the reader that the main clause is delayed.

no comma
He cracks his knuckles *when he's bored*.
(The subordinate clause comes second.)

comma
Even when he sleeps, my noisy brother isn't quiet.
(The subordinate clause comes first.)

Punctuating a poem is usually different from punctuating a sentence; punctuation marks often come only at the ends of the lines of a poem. Challenge students to rewrite the model poem on page 73 in sentences, punctuating the subordinate clauses correctly.

Topic Variations

You can change the topic of the poem to focus on favorite people and things. Students can write "Time" poems about:

- a favorite sports team.
- a favorite musician.
- a favorite car.

Writing About Literature

Students can compose "Time" poems based on the events from a memoir or novel, such as

- Tim's experiences with the Revolutionary War in America in *My Brother Sam Is Dead.*
- Jiang's experiences during the Cultural Revolution in China in *Red Scarf Girl.*

Collier, J., & Collier, C. (1998). *My Brother Sam Is Dead.* New York: Scholastic.

Jiang, J. (1998). *Red Scarf Girl.* New York: Harper Trophy.

We Moved About a Week Ago
by Jack Prelutsky

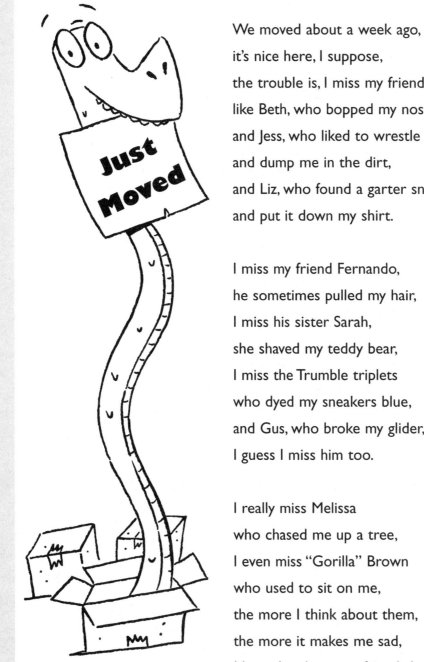

We moved about a week ago,	1
it's nice here, I suppose,	2
the trouble is, I miss my friends,	3
like Beth, who bopped my nose,	4
and Jess, who liked to wrestle	5
and dump me in the dirt,	6
and Liz, who found a garter snake	7
and put it down my shirt.	8
I miss my friend Fernando,	9
he sometimes pulled my hair,	10
I miss his sister Sarah,	11
she shaved my teddy bear,	12
I miss the Trumble triplets	13
who dyed my sneakers blue,	14
and Gus, who broke my glider,	15
I guess I miss him too.	16
I really miss Melissa	17
who chased me up a tree,	18
I even miss "Gorilla" Brown	19
who used to sit on me,	20
the more I think about them,	21
the more it makes me sad,	22
I hope I make some friends here	23
as great as those I had.	24

© 1990 by Jack Prelutsky.

Teaching Grammar With Perfect Poems for Middle School • Scholastic Teaching Resources

Good Friends Poems

⊠ ⊠ ⊠ ⊠ ⊠ ⊠ **Instructional Objective** ⊠ ⊠ ⊠ ⊠ ⊠ ⊠ ⊠

Students write a "Good Friends" poem that contains nine *who* clauses.

Source Poem: "We Moved About a Week Ago" by Jack Prelutsky (reproducible page 80)

Introductory Activity

Distribute copies of "We Moved About a Week Ago" by Jack Prelutsky. Read the poem once to the class. Ask students to circle the word *who* each time it appears in the poem. Then have students underline or highlight *who* plus the phrase that follows and finishes the idea. They should underline: *who bopped my nose, who liked to wrestle and dump me in the dirt, who found a garter snake and put it down my shirt, who dyed my sneakers blue, who broke my glider, who chased me up a tree,* and *who used to sit on me*. Read the poem aloud, having the class read the *who* clauses in unison as you read the rest of the lines.

Modeling Activity

Imitate the model poem with "good friends" as the topic. Have students brainstorm a list of wonderful (rather than awful) things that a friend might do. Model how to exaggerate the actions, such as *sings Happy Birthday in 12 languages* and *blows chewing gum into a 3-foot bubble*. Assign each student to write one line beginning with the friend's name followed by "who_____ and _____." Have students pair up briefly and check that their partner has followed the format.

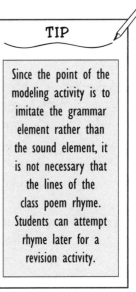

TIP

Since the point of the modeling activity is to imitate the grammar element rather than the sound element, it is not necessary that the lines of the class poem rhyme. Students can attempt rhyme later for a revision activity.

Put everyone's lines together for a class poem. Begin by reading the first three lines from Prelutsky's poem. Then have students take turns reading their lines. End by reading the last two lines from Prelutsky's poem. The class poem could be shared with a local realtor.

Grammar Mini-Lesson

Four ways to define *who* clauses are listed below. Consider which explanations will help your particular students.

Function:

A *who* clause is a dependent or subordinate clause that depends on the main clause or the kernel sentence to function. A subordinate clause begins with a subordinate conjunction. In this poem the subordinate conjunction is *who*, and the subordinate clause functions as an adjective that modifies the proper noun. *Who* clauses are adjective clauses. *Who* clauses follow a noun.

I miss my friends like Beth, *who bopped my nose.*   *subordinate clause*

The addition of a subordinate clause to a main clause creates a complex sentence. Without being attached to the main clause, the subordinate clause is incomplete and is not even considered to be a sentence. A subordinate clause by itself is considered to be a fragment.

Meaning:

Subordinate clauses carry extra information not contained in the main clause. Subordinate conjunctions do not just add information; they indicate a relationship among ideas. Beginning writers can use subordinate clauses to help them avoid fragments and run-ons. Advanced writers can use subordinate clauses to express complex ideas.

Identification:

The best way to spot a subordinate clause is to look for a subordinate conjunction such as *who*. Other subordinate conjunctions that can begin an adjective clause are: *whom, which, that.* These subordinate conjunctions are called relative pronouns because they relate the information back to the noun that they modify. A subordinate clause can be dropped from a sentence, and the main clause will still make sense without it. If the element begins with a subordinate conjunction and can be dropped, it is a subordinate clause.

I miss my friends like Beth, ~~who bopped my nose~~.
The *subordinate clause* can be dropped.

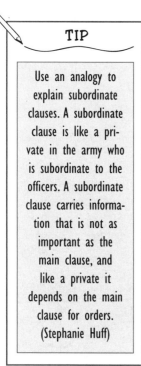

TIP

Use an analogy to explain subordinate clauses. A subordinate clause is like a private in the army who is subordinate to the officers. A subordinate clause carries information that is not as important as the main clause, and like a private it depends on the main clause for orders. (Stephanie Huff)

Example:
Have students review the subordinate clauses in Prelutsky's poem: *who bopped my nose, who liked to wrestle and dump me in the dirt, who found a garter snake and put it down my shirt, who dyed my sneakers blue, who broke my glider, who chased me up a tree,* and *who used to sit on me.*

Prewriting for an Individual Pattern Poem

Students can write their own "Good Friends" poems for friends of their choice. As a class, brainstorm a list of friendly actions. Help students think beyond monetary generosity to activities involving intelligence, volunteerism, artistic talents, and leadership. Ask students to select 11 or more actions and have them list details about each action.

Writing the Poem

Have students draft their own poems, imitating the repeating *who* clause pattern of the original model. Use the frame on page 84 as a guide.

Publishing Activity: Moving Van Book

- Draw or trace a side view of a van on a large rectangular envelope so that the envelope flap is at the tail of the van (recycled catalogue or advertising envelopes work well).

- Trace wheels onto black paper, cut out, and attach with brads.

- Color the van and label it with stickers.

- Print the poem on paper and slide in one side.

TIP

For consistency, more *who* clauses have been added to the second stanza.

Poem Frame

We moved about a week ago,	1
It's nice here, I suppose,	2
the trouble is, I miss my friends,	3
like _____, who _____,	4
(name) (action)	
and _____, who _____	5
(name) (action)	
and _____,	6
(action)	
and _____, who _____	7
(name) (action)	
and _____.	8
(action)	
I miss my friend _____,	9
(name)	
who _____,	10
(action)	
I miss his/her friend _____,	11
(name)	
who _____,	12
(action)	
I miss _____,	13
(name)	
who _____,	14
(action)	
and _____, who _____	15
(name) (action)	
I guess I miss him/her too.	16
I really miss _____,	17
(name)	
who _____,	18
(action)	
I even miss _____,	19
(name)	
who _____,	20
(action)	
the more I think about them,	21
the more it makes me sad,	22
I hope I make some friends here	23
as great as those I had.	24

Critical-Thinking Time

The thought teasers are provided for your students to discuss in small groups and then share with the whole class for further wondering and discussion.

- In the first four lines of the second stanza, Prelutsky varies his pattern and does not include *who* clauses. How does this affect the poem in terms of rhythm and speed? Rewrite these lines to include *who* clauses. (*I miss my friend Fernando, who sometimes pulled my hair. I miss his sister Sarah, who shaved my teddy bear.*)

- Adjective clauses can also begin with *that* and *which*. *Who* is used for people and *that* and *which* are used for animals, objects, and ideas. *That* is used for critical information, and *which* is used for less critical information and takes a comma. Rewrite the first two lines in the last stanza to focus on an object being lost. (*Possible answers: I really miss my computer that had my only copy of my homework. I really miss my computer, which was an older model.*)

- Write two guesses for a Clue game using *who*. (*A possible answer: I suspect Colonel Mustard who is in the den with a knife.*)

Grammar Reinforcement Activity

Use the following activity to reinforce the function of subordinate clauses beginning with *who* and provide an opportunity to discuss additional information or confusing features.

In the game Who Is the Famous Person? students work in small groups to quickly write subordinate clauses that describe famous people. To prepare, collect newspapers and magazines that have images of popular stars in music, TV, the movies, and sports. Divide the class into four teams and give the teams scissors, glue, five large index cards, and a sheet of scrap paper. Have each group create game cards by cutting out pictures of five famous people and gluing the pictures onto the index cards. Have them label these five game cards with a complete sentence: [*Name of star*] *is a famous person*. Then have each group trade their set of cards with another group. Have groups appoint a scribe to record their answers on the scrap paper. On your count, give teams one minute to create and write down five sentences that describe each of the famous people pictured. They must use subordinate clauses beginning with *who* to earn a point (*Madonna is a singer who is also a yoga expert.*). The group with the most correct *who* clauses wins that round. Have groups switch card sets and play again. To increase difficulty, have students write compound *who* clauses.

Grammar Extension Activity

An additional concept about *who* clauses can be introduced to students who are ready to learn more, or this activity can be used for an extra-credit assignment.

When to Use Commas With a *Who* Clause:
Who clauses follow a noun and often take commas before and after because they usually provide nonessential information.

comma   I really miss Melissa, who chased me up a tree.
commas   Melissa, who chased me up a tree, lives in my old town.

However, it is possible for *who* clauses to provide essential information that is needed to keep the main clause from being confusing.

no comma   I cannot find the band member who has my hat.

In this case only the band member with the hat is needed. The who clause does not take commas since it doesn't just modify band member, it specifies the only band member who is needed. In a poem, authors have more freedom to punctuate their lines to keep a desired rhythm. Challenge students to rewrite the poem in sentences, punctuating the who clauses correctly.

Topic Variations

You can change the assignment to focus on different types of people. Students can write poems about:

• good teachers.
• unusual neighbors.
• unusual relatives.

Writing About Literature

Students can compose "Good Friends" poems based on characters in a novel, such as

• the neighbors in Cleveland in *Seedfolks*.
• Jake's many new friends in *Jake, Reinvented*.

Fleischman, P. (2004). *Seedfolks.* New York: Harper Trophy.

Korman, G. (2005). *Jake, Reinvented.* New York: Hyperion.

Supporting Language Learning Beyond the Grammar Lessons in This Book

We teachers are interested not only in what works, but also in why it works. In this chapter, you'll find some of the broader theories about language learning that have helped me to develop the grammar lessons in this book—and that may help you to develop new methods for language arts instruction in your own classroom. I address four guiding questions about language instruction and how research supports nontraditional approaches. For each question, I mention some practical applications and cite scholars whose work may inspire you and inform your practice. References are included on page 92.

How can we build on students' natural language learning?

No matter how many times I read what literacy expert Frank Smith has to say about how children learn language, I am amazed by how much children learn before they come to school. In *Understanding Reading* (1994), Smith says that children "invent grammar," meaning that each child "discovers" the grammar system through trial and error. Smith describes the process of learning to speak as hypothesis testing, feedback evaluation, and theory construction; errors are an important part of the process of learning complex language rules.

Children's speech is full of examples of grammar "mistakes" that are evidence of their growing understanding of language. For example, linguist Constance Weaver (1996) explains how errors like *goed* instead of *went* reveal that a child is intuitively inventing the past-tense rule for *-ed* ending regular verbs. Children become increasingly facile with language as they practice speaking and later, writing. Brian Cambourne's work with early literacy emphasizes that the child's first attempts are global approximations, but with later performances, the child's language eventually becomes more

MAKING INSTRUCTION A LEARNING PROCESS FOR YOU, THE TEACHER
When you finally get a strategy to work after trying it repeatedly and changing this or that, ask yourself, what made the method work? Think about your process metacognitively. If you can articulate why a particular strategy worked, then you can likely invent other strategies based on what you've discovered.

detailed and exact (1998). The challenge becomes how to respect errors as a part of developmental growth rather than condemn them as signs of total ignorance.

The key, I believe, is to tap students' intuitive knowledge about grammar and let them wonder about language through discussion with their peers and teacher. In the grammar lessons I've included here, I use the Critical-Thinking Time activities to help students consciously theorize about how language works (*Is the pattern the same in each line of the poem?*). A great way to use these prompts is to have a weekly 15-minute "language lab" session in which students analyze a language pattern or convention within real texts, using a discovery process of asking and then answering their own questions. Of course, there are many ways to set up this language lab session—from small group work to individual response notebooks that are shared to partner discussions that feed into whole-class discussions. The idea is to create an atmosphere of wondering in your classroom that lets students actively make sense of how language works.

How can we help students take even greater control of their language learning?

When I started teaching, I had been taught to discourage any social interaction among my students to avoid "distractions" from teaching. After reading the theories of cognitive psychologist Lev Vygotsky (1986), I began to understand the critical importance of social interaction to all learning. Educational scholars now use Vygotsky's notion of the zone of proximal development (1978) to explain how a student's intelligence can be increased with slight assistance from a teacher or another student. The mentor provides a supportive scaffold to guide the student's performance with the least intervention possible. This scaffolding approach requires a lot of social dialogue to question, extend students' ideas further, and get feedback from learners so the mentor can help them progress.

Other Vygotskian concepts are equally useful for educators. Vygotsky's work on inner speech (1986) maps out how social talk eventually becomes internalized as thought processes. In the same way we introduce students to math concepts with models and concrete manipulatives, we must also introduce language concepts through purposeful talk before we can expect students to internalize the abstract labels. Consider the amount of time you allow students to discuss new language concepts before you ask them to apply the concept in their writing. Is it enough? Have you allowed time for them to figure out how they already use it or how it might help them communicate? (See the critical thinking discussion above and on page 6.)

One of Vygotsky's most important areas of study was high-level thought processes. He believed that these thought processes enable human beings to adapt to the environment by increasing their own inner self-regulation or self-control. When we apply this notion to education, our aim is to teach students how to think so that they can control themselves and make the most of their learning experiences. Regrettably, teachers are pressured to monitor students' behavior, marking every error students make while learning. However, controlling students is not the same as teaching them self-control.

We must find ways to help students manage their own writing rather than merely correcting workbook sentences or waiting for the teacher to correct their writing for them. When we support students with good models, guided instruction, choice, and a joyful purpose for communicating, students take responsibility for their writing. They become invested in the product and the real audience with whom it will be shared. My students always request more time and help with proofreading when they care about their writing. This is why the grammar lessons in this book emphasize writing meaningful poetry that is artistically published so that students will be proud to celebrate their writing with others. Consider the different audiences to whom students might present their written work and the types of publication formats that will build excitement and enthusiasm for their writing. Can you create new audiences within the school or bring in families and other community members who may find specific projects interesting? What successful publishing formats do your colleagues use?

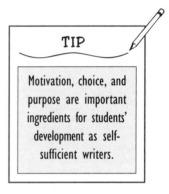

TIP

Motivation, choice, and purpose are important ingredients for students' development as self-sufficient writers.

How can language instruction become more compatible with brain research?

The brain seems to be hardwired to perceive patterns. Research with newborn infants has demonstrated that they prefer patterns that look like faces. Human beings find and create patterns everywhere. Math is taught as numerical patterns. Linguists diagram sentences into schematic trees that look amazingly similar to chemical or mathematical formulas. Artists and musicians create repeated patterns that appeal to our aesthetic sensibility. Our brains recognize patterns after we have gathered enough data from real-life experience. All these patterns—facial, numerical, linguistic, chemical, artistic, musical—help us make sense of the world. In fact, new information only makes sense to us when we can associate it with a pattern that we already know. In other words, unless we can place the new information within an existing pattern, it just doesn't make sense to us and we reject or forget it.

Patterns are essential to learning. When we have no choice but to learn things that do not seem to make any sense to us or do not have an easily recognizable pattern, we associate or link the new learning into a familiar pattern. When we consciously create ways to remember new information by placing it within patterns that we will remember, we create mnemonic devices—medical students use rhymes and visual associations to remember anatomy, and chemical engineers make humorous sentences from the first letters of terms that they need to memorize. Similarly, when our students cannot make sense of particular spelling and grammar conventions, we can encourage them to use memory by association. For instance, students can use mnemonic devices for learning spelling and usage patterns, such as the reminder *principal* has *-pal* at the end because the principal is your pal.

My own breakthrough in teaching came about when I began to think of usage rules as a pattern of language use that society has sanctioned as "preferred." I have come to see that one type of grammar or one dialect is not inherently better than another; language conventions are just accepted habits that change over time. Moreover, what is accepted by the larger society as standard and what is considered substandard is undoubtedly a political choice that has racial, class, and gender implications, which I discuss with my students. As their teacher, I never, never devalue my students' home languages—this is particularly critical because research shows that students may equate a rejection of their home language with a feeling of discomfort and exclusion from school itself (Penrose, 2002). However, I also recognize that my students must learn preferred patterns of language in order to participate fully in the world in which we live. So I teach my students to discover language patterns and to work and play with those patterns, as they do when they imitate and make variations on a model poem. In this way, the patterns become familiar and students gain ownership of them through using them. My goal is for them to gain mastery of "academic" English in addition to their home language, so that they can use both languages effectively for their own purposes.

How can we make grammar instruction fit within the context of meaningful student writing?

If you are interested in learning about the history of language instruction, you will find a great resource in the work of Constance Weaver (1996), who does an excellent job summarizing, discussing, and analyzing several major studies about grammar instruction. Weaver reminds us that as long ago as 1936, the National Council of Teachers of English recommended that grammar no longer be taught separately from writing instruction. Moreover, Weaver explains a great deal about the possibilities for teaching grammar through writing. Of particular use are suggestions to teach grammar and usage in mini-lessons that reflect students' developmental needs as writers. For example, skills such as sentence manipulation need to be taught using both excellent models as well as students' own ideas and writing. In a related anthology volume (1998), Weaver includes many individual approaches to embedding grammar instruction in the writing process.

Using Weaver's and my own research, I have grouped current approaches to teaching grammar in the context of meaningful writing into three categories:

- teaching students to recognize grammar elements and sentence patterns through guided writing assignments
- teaching advanced syntax patterns through sentence combining during revision
- teaching students to correct their own usage errors during editing and proofreading

The lessons in this volume fit mainly into the first category, although there are some editing activities that address usage issues. I recommend using all three of these approaches regularly, provided they are used in the context of real student writing.

A major problem you may encounter with published instructional materials is that these materials tend to isolate language study from students' writing. For example, the second approach, sentence combining, is an excellent way to get students to try out more sophisticated sentence structures; however, sentence-combining activities generally take the form of workbook pages. Materials developed for the third approach, usage mini-lessons, are frequently published as daily writing drills. Using these materials gives teachers a concrete way to cover specific skills and prepare students for taking tests. However, it is an ineffective way to get students to apply what they've learned to their own writing. Error correction just doesn't transfer to improving student writing when it is practiced on phony example sentences.

As a profession, we are only just learning how to move away from workbook pages to find teachable moments during authentic writing practice. Consider ways you can weave instruction based on students' needs, writing interests, and actual written work into your language arts curriculum—ways to achieve meaningful teaching and learning.

PROFESSIONAL SOURCES CITED

Burke, J. (2001). Developing students' textual intelligence through grammar. *Voices from the Middle, 8*(6), 56–61.

Buzan, T. (1983). *Use both sides of your brain.* New York: Dutton.

Cambourne, B. (1988). *The whole story: Natural learning and the acquisition of literacy in the classroom.* New York: Scholastic.

Dixon-Krauss, L. (1996). *Vygotsky in the classroom: Mediated literacy instruction and assessment.* White Plains, NY: Longman.

Jensen, E. (1998). *Teaching with the brain in mind.* Alexandria, VA: Association for Supervision and Curriculum Development.

Mack, N. (1988). Grammar: Site of class conflict. *Focus: Teaching Language Arts, 14*(2), 34–44.

Penrose, A. (2002). Academic literacy perceptions and performance: Comparing first-generation and continuing-generation college students. *Research in the Teaching of English, 36*(4), 437–61.

Smith, F. (1994). *Understanding reading: A psycholinguistic analysis of reading and learning to read.* New York: Holt, Rinehart and Winston.

Vygotsky, L. (1978). *Mind in society: The development of higher psychological processes.* (Cole et al., Eds.). Cambridge, MA: Harvard University Press.

Vygotsky, L. *Thought and language.* (1986). (A. Kozulin, Ed.). Cambridge, MA: MIT Press.

Weaver, C. (1996). *Teaching grammar in context.* Portsmouth, NH: Boynton Cook.

Weaver, C. (1998). *Lessons to share on teaching grammar in context.* Portsmouth, NH: Boynton Cook.

Wolfe, P. (2001). *Brain matters: Translating research into classroom practice.* Alexandria, VA: Association for Supervision and Curriculum Development.

Zebroski, J. T. (1994). *Thinking through theory: Vygotskian perspectives on the teaching of writing.* Portsmouth, NH: Heinemann.

GRAMMAR HANDBOOKS (FROM SIMPLEST TO MOST COMPLEX):

Sebranek, P., Meryer, V., & Kemper, D. (2006). *Writers inc.* Burlington, WI: Write Source.

Hacker, D. (2007). *A pocket style manual.* New York: Bedford St. Martin's.

Harris, M. (2007). *The Prentice Hall reference guide to grammar and usage.* Upper Saddle River, NJ: Prentice Hall.

Kolln, M. (1995). *Understanding English grammar.* New York: Macmillan.

Lunsford, A., & Connors, R. (2003). *The St. Martin's handbook.* New York: Bedford St. Martin's.

Rice, S. (1993). *Right words, right places.* Belmont, CA: Wadsworth.

Bernstein, T. (1995). *The careful writer.* New York: Free Press.

MORE RESOURCES

For additional photographs of the grammar projects in this book, and to contact Nancy Mack, please visit her Web site at www.wright.edu/~nancy.mack

TIP

If you're looking for inexpensive or free grammar handbooks for your class, you might try calling a local university or community college and asking the English professors to donate handbooks or collect them from students who may no longer need them. Although usage conventions change very slowly, new editions come out frequently and the old editions decrease significantly in monetary value.

YOUNG ADULT LITERATURE CITED

Avi. (1992). *The true confessions of Charlotte Doyle*. New York: Harper Trophy.

Choldenko, G. (2004). *Al Capone does my shirts*. New York: Puffin.

Collier, J., & Collier, C. (1998). *My brother Sam is dead*. New York: Scholastic.

Crutcher, C. (2004). *Ironman*. New York: Harper Teen.

Fleischman, P. (2004). *Seedfolks*. New York: Harper Trophy.

Fleischman, P. (1999). *Whirligig*. New York: Laurel Leaf Press.

Hesse, K. (1999). *Out of the dust*. New York: Scholastic.

Howe, N. (2000). *The adventures of blue avenger*. New York: Harper.

Jiang, J. (1998). *Red scarf girl*. New York: Harper Trophy.

Johnson, A. (1994). *Toning the sweep*. New York: Scholastic.

Korman, G. (2005). *Jake, reinvented*. New York: Hyperion.

Lowry, L. (2002). *The giver*. New York: Laurel Leaf Press.

O'Dell, S. (1971). *Island of the blue dolphins*. New York: Dell Yearling.

Paulsen, G. (1996). *Hatchet*. New York: Aladdin.

Peck, R. (2000). *A long way from Chicago*. New York: Puffin.

Peck, R. (2002). *A year down yonder*. New York: Puffin.

Rowling, J. K. (1999). *Harry Potter and the sorcerer's stone*. New York: Scholastic.

Spinelli, J. (2002). *Maniac Magee*. New York: Scholastic.

Voigt, C. (2003). *Dicey's song*. New York: Aladdin.

Yolen, J., & Harris, R. (2001). *Queen's own fool*. New York: Putnam.

INDEX

NOTES